Poetically Speaking
- A Poetic Tale of My Life -

LaTarsia "Targie" Taylor

Copyright 2010 © By LaTarsia "Targie" Taylor

Street Money Publishing, LLC
P.O. Box 672214
Bronx, NY 10467
Local: (718) 515-BOOK
E-mail: info@streetmoneypublishing.com

Printed in the United States. All rights reserved. No parts of this book may be used or reproduced in any manner whatsoever without prior written permission from the publisher except in the case of brief quotations embodied in critical reviews and articles.

"Today," "Mommy's Gone To Heaven," "In Loving Memory of My Step-Dad," "Ooh, Darkskin Brotha," "The Oak Tree," "Mommy's Gone Now," "Just Don't Want to be Lonely," "My Sister," were used by permission of the Authors.

All Scripture quotations are taken from the King James Version of the Bible.

First Print: 9/2010

Library of Congress Control Number: 2009941053
ISBN-10: 0-9793724-6-1
ISBN-13: 978-0-9793724-6-9

You can also order via: **www.targietaylor.com**

Web Design
Christopher K. Wright – www.ablemindz.com

Photography
Gregg Richards – www.tryating.com

Model
LaTarsia "Targie" Taylor

Cover Design
Leap Graphics, Ltd. – www.leapgraphics.com

In Loving Memory

of My Mommy,

Brenda Taylor-Golds

Acknowledgements

This book of poetry is dedicated to "You," all of my supporters. I would like to thank God first and foremost because without Him where would I be? I thank God for keeping me and saving me when I was supposed to be dead a number of times, but God. Umm huh "Can't nobody do me like Jesus!"

In recognition of your love and support, I would like to thank my sisters LaToya, LeChema, Sierra & Kim for being there to listen and allowing me to get on their nerves sometimes. I love you. To my nephews Rai-Shaun, Ray-Quan, Rah-Quell, Rai-Vaughn, and Ryan also my nieces Kia, Karin, Kahlia, and finally Jala. I love you so much. Every time I would get low in my spirit and cried for a child, one of you were conceived. I thank God for sending all of you right on time.

I want to thank my Pastor, Bishop Lillian Robinson-Wiltshire for never giving up on me and teaching the word of God in fullness and in truth. I love you.

To my family members and friends who are too many to name all over the United States of America. I love you. We have had our ups and downs, but we have overcome a lot of drama and some good and bad days, but thank God we are here.

Also to all the people who took me in when I was living from pillow to post, thank you so much and I love you so. You really are appreciated.

A special thanks to SMP, may God continue to bless and keep you in His unchanging hands. I love you all.

Preface

This book tells a story through poems. Please do not judge me, because I am only human. You will see that some of the poems are inspirational, sad, angry, religious, or worldly. I am saved, but have backslid down through the years. I have searched for love in all the wrong places. This book is about maturing and going through the ups and downs, trials and tribulations of life. There are poems from different walks of life. I hope this book gives you something to think about in your own life. There are parts where I think I was dumb as hell, but that's why we live and learn from our mistakes. We cannot dwell on the past. We have to live for today and try to keep God first so that our road may be blessed tomorrow. It is too easy to fall into temptation, and hard to fall out of it. It is too easy to say, "God I love you and I will serve you always." When tragedy hits home we either lose faith in God or run to Him. I believe that a just man does fall, but he will rise again in the name of Jesus by the power of the Holy Spirit. I started writing these poems when I was 16 years old. I have grown from a loved child to a struggling teen, into a well-fed woman, and I thank God for bringing me this far.

LaTarsia "Targie" Taylor

It Gets Greater Later - 11/14/2008

So the storm has come, and washed away your smile,

So the tears continuously fall, but it's only for awhile,

Your money may be low, and your bills are sky high,

Do you know God is waiting for you to give him a try?

You've been through the hurt, misery, and pain,

Learning and growing, for it was not in vain,

You are a living testimony for all those going through,

So stand tall, walk proud, and know that God loves you,

Don't wait until it's too late, God will give you a full plate,

Don't mind all the haters, because it gets greater later!

Let go, and let God, believe me it's not that hard.

Scripture Reference(s)

John 3:16 · Ecclesiastes 3:1 - 8 · Psalm 51:9 - 15

Poetically Speaking

Dear God - 11/30/2008

*My body is weary, and my mind is worn,
It seems the more I try, everything goes wrong,
I want to live for you, with Christ in me,
Not just talking, but walking in victory,
Where people will see your light in my eyes,
A change so intense, they want to give you a try,
Change my heart Lord, let my heart be true,
I need you in my life, I can't live without you,
Your power is great, I submit myself unto you,
I will resist the devil and he will flee from me too,
I want you to clean up my life, so I can live,
I need your hand Lord, my heart to you I give,
I'm tired of sin, I'm tired of unclean things,
Lord encourage my soul and let me sing,
Glory hallelujah, I give you the highest praise,
You are magnificent, almighty, my everything,
Who can save me, who can restore my peace?
Who will love me? Only you God unconditionally,
I stand in need, please Lord have mercy on me,
Forgive me for my sins, cleanse me from within,
Save me Jesus, my savior and my King of Kings,
You are the way, the truth, and the life, my everything,
Fill me with the Holy Spirit, as my new life begins,
God you are my doctor, my lawyer, my friend,
God you are never changing, and omnipotent,
God you are my beginning and you are my end.*

Scripture Reference(s)

Romans 7:19 · James 4:7 · Hebrews 11:1 · Hebrews 2 · Hebrews 12:1

LaTarsia "Targie" Taylor

<u>Help Is Just A Whisper Away</u> - 11/30/2008

If you would let God in your life,
He'll be there right by your side,

If you are down to your last cry,
Get down on your knees tonight,

Say yes to your greatest opportunity,
Because God will give you the victory,

I know that God will see you through,
Because your Father really loves you,

Ask for help, strength and guidance,
With a pure heart to love and forgive,

Knowledge and wisdom to understand,
The mystery of the gospel & God's plan,

With your makeover you are renewed,
Peace be still and may God bless you.

<u>Scripture Reference(s) - A Renewed Mind</u>

Romans 8:24 - 28 · Romans 12:1 - 3

Poetically Speaking

What's Going On? – 12/12/2008

I asked for peace,
And it seemed like hell,
I asked for strength,
And my energy failed,
I asked for deliverance,
And my addictions got worse,
But Jesus is my Savior
And I will stay in church,
Yes I know through it all,
I may slip, stumble & fall,
But God won't give me
Anything I can't handle,
I know I can make it
Through traps & scandals,
For after the rain
The sun will shine,
Yes after the pain
The God in me shall rise.

Scripture Reference(s) - Trials & Tribulations

James 1

LaTarsia "Targie" Taylor

A Barren Woman - 1/2009

The bible says, blessed is a barren woman,
But it feels like a curse,
You try hard and pray, you try to understand,
But this emptiness hurts,
The doctor says, you are fertile as they come,
Why aren't you with child?
To God you pray, years ago you miscarried one,
But you were young and wild,
This world is so evil, so being without children
Might not be so bad,
Some people worry and go through hell with
The children they have,
So I thank you God, because only you know
The stories that remain untold,
I have you God, my family and friends to
Fill in that deep empty hole.

Scripture Reference(s)

Isaiah 54:1 - 10

Poetically Speaking

May God Watch Between Us - 4/8/2009

May God bless you more and more.

May God keep you safe in his arms,

May peace be still,

And may your heart stay true,

Because no matter what,

I have a lot of love for you,

May God guide our way,

As we live for today,

May God encourage our souls,

As we plan our future goals,

May God teach us how to live,

How to give all we can give,

So that we can hold on,

Through every storm,

Trusting in God and pressing on.

Scripture Reference(s)

Matthew 22:37

LaTarsia "Targie" Taylor

I Am Torn – 5/3/2009

I am torn between what's real and fake,
I am torn with my weary heart at stake,
What should I do, how shall I respond?
If only I could see the future & beyond,

Half of me says yes & the other says no,
What is from God? How will I know?
The pit that I am in, slowly sinking away,
I want to climb out, but I can't see the way,

What is right and what is wrong?
Why am I confused? How can I hold on?
Through God's unchanging hand,
I will rise from sinking sand,

And in due time I will see what's right,
As long as I stand, God will show me the light.

Scripture Reference(s) – For the Soul

Psalm 27

Poetically Speaking

To The Mothers That Helped - 4/4/2009

Thank you for stepping up to the plate,
Being like a mom, while mine is in Heaven's gate,
Thank you for putting up with my teenage years,
I was a handful, but now I listen, see, and hear,

Thank you for accepting me, and never judging me,
With your advice and guidance I have taken heed,
Thank you for laughing at most of my jokes,
I know some of them were crazy to you older folks,

But you loved me anyhow, and never abused my heart,
I know Mommy is proud that you stood to fill her part,
I love you for keeping it real,
May God bless you and peace be still.

LaTarsia "Targie" Taylor

To My Grandmothers - 4/4/2009

Thank you for trying to guide me

In the right direction,

Thank you for being tough,

Giving me strength, love and affection,

There were times

When I thought you were being cruel,

But I have learned that discipline enforces the rules,

We've had our ups and downs, yes our highs and lows,

You have opened your doors,

When I had no place to go,

We have overcome many trials and obstacles,

I thank you for caring, and yes I do love you too,

So may God bless you and may peace be still,

A Grandmother's love is special and ever so real.

Poetically Speaking

<u>For My Auntie Sheree - 4/4/2009</u>

You are so quiet and unique,
You have a peace within you,
Which makes you easy to love,
You are the greatest Auntie too,
Sent from Heaven above,
So quiet and gentle,
Handle with care,
So refined,
But you always lend your ear,
You would listen to my stories,
And gasp in shock, feeling sorry,
But still you would never judge me,
You didn't like when I cursed carefree,
You would take my hand and pop me,
That is funny, because I am on my own,
Auntie did you forget I am grown?
Don't ever change Auntie, keep it real,
I love you, God bless you, and peace be still.

LaTarsia "Targie" Taylor

Uncle I Miss You

I remember the times when we were close like glue,
You were always around, cool, fun, and caring too,
Circumstances and distance has separated our family,
Where did we go wrong? I know prayer comes in handy,

"A family that prays together stays together,"
So let's give it a try, we will be like the weather,
Shining, raining, and storming too,
In spite of it all we'll make it through,

Dedicated to my Uncle Jeffrey, but I would like to show some love to all of my uncles. Love, peace, and hair grease!

Poetically Speaking

The Power Of Our Lord - 4/5/2009

Broken, but now I am whole,

Vengeful, but now I let go,

Sickly, but now I am healed,

Empty, but now I am filled,

Imprisoned, but now I am free,

Jesus gave me victory,

When I was blind

God gave me sight,

I know with him,

I will be all right,

Jesus died on cavalry,

Just to set me free,

So I know I will have peace.

Scripture Reference(s) – Healing

Jeremiah 30 • Psalm 71 • Isaiah 53:5

LaTarsia "Targie" Taylor

A Word From Our Ancestors - 7/8/2009

It's been a long time coming
And we have come a long way
From our motherland,
Traded and deceived becoming
American slaves
Slaughtered, beaten & raped,
We've done took all we can take,
In this land we have shed blood,
Tears & sweat,
In this land built from our strength,
But we don't get any respect,
No thank you or credit
But God is all knowing
He has seen our tears
God has heard our cries,
So my child don't you fear,
God will carry you by and by,
As my spirit, yes my soul
Watches over you,
Seeing and living through you too,
You will grow my children strong and mighty,
You will be brave and blessed highly,
We have paved the way for you to press on
Kings and Queens are where you are from,
My Princes & Princesses your day has come
So open your eyes, use your head
Our flesh is buried, but our souls
Aren't dead,
Stand up and be the men & women
That you are
Don't give up, stand tall, and reach for the stars,
Press on my children, for it's

Poetically Speaking

<u>A Word From Our Ancestors – 7/8/2009</u>
(continued)

Only a matter of time,
We will reach the sky,
Struggling & strengthening
The ties that bind
We are connected by blood, and bonded by love,
So peace be still
Angels are watching from here and
Heaven above…

LaTarsia "Targie" Taylor

My Sister – 7/9/2009

My sister I love you!
So glad to have you here,
Every day I think of you
& always know you're near,

My sister I love you!
Even though I don't call every day,
You're always on my mind,
Knowing you are in my life,
I know everything is fine,

My sister I love you!
You are the best sister I could ever have,
I can't think about you not being here,
Because in my heart there's so much fear,

My sister I love you
And forever I will,
Thank you God,
And peace be still.

Dedicated to me by my sister, Sierra.

Poetically Speaking

To My Sister Sierra Locke - 7/9/2009

My sister I love you too,
You are special and beautiful,
Don't let anyone let you down,
Remember that I am here in town,

So pick up your head,
Walk tall and proud,
You are a princess
God's blessed child,

So when the storm comes,
Stand still don't run,
God will show you the way,
My little sister just pray,

People take your kindness for weakness,
Your anger for rudeness,
But God knows your heart
So keep on don't stop,
A lovely rose true indeed,
My sister, my dear, you are free...

I love you baby girl. All my sisters are my world.

LaTarsia "Targie" Taylor

Dear Michael Jackson – 8/3/2009

May the world leave you be,
So you can rest in peace,
May God hold you up high in the sky,
So people can stop judging,
And asking why,
You have left an unbeatable trail,
Every time someone tries they only fail,
You are one of the greatest, believe me,
Your talent is appreciated,
So float on,
And "I'll be There" holding on,
Until the end of time,
Because it doesn't matter,
If it's "Black or White"
This is "Thriller," thriller night,
And "We are the World,"
We are the children,
So I will strive hard to make it in,
Because I'm looking at the "Man in the Mirror",
And I'm asking him to change his ways."
So I love you MJ,
And I'm gonna make a change,
Rest in peace,
Yes, yes, in heavenly sleep.

Poetically Speaking

My Sisters – 8/7/2009

Words cannot express the love I have for you,
But my actions really describe how much I do,
My sisters the trials from which we came,
The bond that ties us so no one can gain
Entrance in our world painted by love,
Only God knows in Heaven above,

There is nothing that can tear us apart,
Some tried, but we are three in one heart,
My sisters my blood, my Mommy's joy,
I can't express myself, boy oh boy,

I pray that God keeps us strong,
So we can conquer every storm,
I pray that God will keep our ties,
I pray that God blesses us by and by,

Thank you for loving me through it all,
Thank you for always being there on call
Every time I needed you regardless of what,
You held my hand, and even kicked my butt,
Every smile and tear that we have shed,
We are a family and God is our Head.

Toya & Chema, yes I love you. Our bond shall always last.
You are the keys to my future and you know my past.

LaTarsia "Targie" Taylor

Stronger Than An Ox-Dana

Through the thunder and rain
Overcoming sickness and pain,
You are still yet holding on
Your amazing strength is born,
A queen, more than a conqueror
Yes that's what you are,
May God continue to keep you
As Macker kisses the stars,
Stay strong and don't let go
You are an inspirational rose,
Growing, sprouting, learning
Teaching, preaching, and yearning,
For a better you, and a better me
You are beautiful my sister & deep,
Forever bonded you and me
Love, peace, and hair grease...

Poetically Speaking

♦♥♦

About *"Stronger Than An Ox"*

Dedicated to Dana Scott in the loss of Wanda (Macker) her mom. I wish I would have stuck to my word and visited you all sooner. Life is too short to keep putting off visiting family & friends.

♦♥♦

LaTarsia "Targie" Taylor

♦♥♦

The story of my past begins:

The next first four poems were written while I was in a psychiatric ward. I was 16 years old and by the grace of God I survived an attempted suicide.

♦♥♦

Poetically Speaking

<u>Life - 5/14/1990</u>

A time of living,
A time of death,
Which is more dreadful?
No one knows,
There are many roads,
In life you stumble & fall,
Sometimes you go straight,
But with death,
There is no escape,
No one knows what it's like
On the other side,
Only if you are an angel
From the heavenly skies,
Would you like to be dead or alive?
Think about it,
There's no repentance after suicide,
Just suck it up and be strong,
God will bring you through every storm.

LaTarsia "Targie" Taylor

My Cold - 5/15/1990

Like a cobweb it caught me by surprise,

I couldn't move my arms,

And it hurt to open my eyes,

It stayed with me for quite a while,

Like a mother who doesn't want

To abandon her child,

My legs were weak,

And goose bumps appeared,

My doggone stomach ached,

And my pounding heart you could hear,

But now it's gone,

Whew it left me alone,

I guess it went to visit

Someone else's home.

Poetically Speaking

Lonely Girl - 5/29/1990

She was so happy,

She had everything a girl could have,

Then the trials came & separated her from her Mommy,

And she received a broken heart after that,

Things that a teen should not have to deal with,

Was thrown her way,

Everybody said, "Just hold on and pray,"

Everyone pointed fingers judging her,

The poor girl's mind was in a blur,

Where was the love and respect?

Why didn't anybody give a heck?

Now the poor girl has committed suicide,

Now everyone is asking why oh why?

Now everyone wants to show their love,

But where were they when all she needed was a hug?

LaTarsia "Targie" Taylor

It's The Medication - 6/30/1990

My head is spinning I can't feel a thing,
Oops I fell and I lost my dang on swing,
It's not me it's the medication,
I'm here receiving hospitalization,

I'm walking in circles scratching my head,
Looking like a zombie from the living dead,
It's not me, blame it on the medication,
I'm drugged up it's not a good sensation,

You forget most of the bad times,
The drug takes a lot off your mind,
Maybe a little too much,
You took a shower,
Oops you forgot to wash up,
It's not you, it's the medication,
Remember you are receiving hospitalization.

Poetically Speaking

◆♥◆

About "It's The Medication"

After reading this poem, you may think otherwise, but just for the record I was not drugged up. My Grandmother signed the papers for me not to receive any kind of medication, except for the iron pills. I wrote this poem because of the people I had seen walking around in there. Some of them really looked like they had lost their minds. I did have some good times on the ward. If anybody knows me or has crossed paths with me, you know that I am a people person. I will have a conversation with almost anyone.

◆♥◆

LaTarsia "Targie" Taylor

Emotionally Devoted To You - 8/11/1990

I tried to let go,

but I just couldn't,

My mind would say, "Yes,"

but my heart wouldn't,

It seems like there is nothing else to do,

Because I'm emotionally devoted to you,

My heart defends you

Even when you're wrong,

That is what keeps me

Constantly holding on,

Our love could be false or maybe it's true,

Because I'm emotionally devoted to you.

Poetically Speaking

Just Don't Want To Be Lonely - 9/29/1990

*Come share my love,
Let's take a walk in the park,
You can push as I swing,
Happiness & joy you'll bring,
Grab my hand and hold me,
I just don't want to be lonely,
You can stay tonight,
And the next day if you can,
You can kiss me,
And do what's best,
Because I'm your woman,
And you are my man,
When you go out,
Leave a number with me,
I'm not possessive,
I just don't want to be lonely.*

This poem was dedicated to me by my first carnal love. I know *now* that God is my first love and I was never lonely because God was always there with me and He will never leave or forsake me.

LaTarsia "Targie" Taylor

Today

Today was just another day,
An ordinary one,
The rain and clouds appeared,
Chasing away the sun,

Today went by without
The slightest cause for cheer,
Your face I did not see,
And your voice I did not hear,

Today I sit in a whirlpool of sorrow,
But maybe we will meet
If not today then tomorrow,

Today I sit with scattered emotions,
Close to tears,
It's not the thought of having you,
It's the thought of losing you I fear.

Oh, that was so sweetly written by my first carnal love in November of 1990.

You Were Cheating - 11/11/1990

Now things are visa versa,
If anyone's hurt,
It will be me who hurts ya,

Don't think I'm going to let it go,
'Cause I'm not,
It's just that now I run the show,
And hold my heart,

It's hard for me to trust anyone now,
I refuse to cry,
Don't ask me how I can feel this way
You know why.

LaTarsia "Targie" Taylor

Part of Me - 11/11/1990

You caught me off guard,
I was so confused,
How could I tell my family
I was carrying you?
Sometimes I sit & wonder
Thinking about you,
What if you were born?
But it's too late,
My baby forever gone,
I hope you forgive me,
For what I have done,
But I was scared,
I was too young,
I didn't think I could live
Up to my responsibilities,
I barely knew your daddy
Right now I'm so hurt,
But I won't let it show,
Oh baby, why did I let you go?
You will always be,
A special part of me.

Poetically Speaking

◆♥◆

About *"Part of Me"*

This poem is not about me. I had a friend in high school that had an abortion who was very distraught. I wrote this poem so she could release her feelings. I just closed my eyes and put myself in her shoes and came up with this.

◆♥◆

LaTarsia "Targie" Taylor

<u>Mommy's Gone Now - 1/17/1991</u>

It's never too late to say I love you,

Especially to a woman so lovely and true,

Even though you lie there with no breath at all,

I can feel your stare Mommy it's you who I call,

Yes I want you near me forever and a day,

But Mom for some reason the Lord took you away,

Maybe it's best that you've departed from us,

I will be strong for God I trust,

I may not be able to touch you or hear you speak,

But Mommy I'll always love you,

Because you're a part of me.

Love Always,
Targie & Chema

Poetically Speaking

♦♥♦

About "Mommy's Gone Now"

My Mommy died on January 13, 1991. Before her demise, she received most of her heart's desires. She gave her life back to God. Then God gave her a home, a husband, her children and the love that she needed to get by.

♦♥♦

LaTarsia "Targie" Taylor

Mommy's Gone To Heaven - 1/17/1991

My Mommy's gone to Heaven
And that's no doubt
She's gone to praise the Lord
She's gone to laugh and shout
See my Mommy accepted the
Lord as her personal Savior
For she had the most extreme
The most extreme behavior
See I know my mother
Committed many sins
But she still had her faith and
Trust within Him
My Mommy may not have had
Houses or wealth
My Mommy may not have had
Cars or a $15,000 dress
But my Mommy had her
Children and has the Lord
And you know people my Mommy
Is blessed and better than blessed
And yes my Mommy has gone to Heaven.

Written by: LaToya Taylor

Poetically Speaking

<u>*Peace Be Still* - 1/24/1991</u>

Peace be still in Mommy's heart,

Because if loves in it Mommy was a part,

She always had a pretty smile,

She brightened your day,

Like a newborn child,

No matter how blue you were,

She made you smile,

Lifting your spirits up,

May peace be still in Mommy's soul,

She was talented,

Funny and most of all bold,

Most importantly Mommy was blessed,

And a woman like that is hard to forget,

So may peace be still.

LaTarsia "Targie" Taylor

<u>My Lord, My Lord – 3/4/1991</u>

My burden is heavy,
My good days don't last,
My life seems endless,
Every day is the past,

Help my family to cope,
Help me to change,
I have reached the end,
Should I jump or hang?

Lift up my spirit,
Turn my soul around,
Lift me up Lord,
I won't utter a sound,

I have faith in you,
God I trust you too,
Help me to go on,
What am I to do?

Poetically Speaking

About "My Lord, My Lord"

After this poem I didn't write for almost a year. Well, if I did I don't have the notebooks. I know after my Mommy's death I lost my way. I did a lot of things to release the pain. I stopped loving myself and was rebellious towards God and open to the world. That was when Shauntasia was born mentally, and Targie died spiritually.

♦♥♦

LaTarsia "Targie" Taylor

<u>Absent Mom or Dad - 6/1991</u>

I didn't ask to be here,
So why are you neglecting me?
You are suppose to care,
Shoot I didn't plant my seed,

So what you are separated,
Why are you ignoring me?
Making me feel unappreciated,
Lost, alone, and incomplete,

I am still your child,
Regardless of how you feel,
Circumstances make you wild,
But there were condoms, foam, and pills,

You chose your bed,
Now wake up & pay your dues,
I won't suffer long,
Because God keeps me strong,
And God's love is true.

♦♥♦

Thank you for bringing me in this world, even though you were in and out of my life, I still love you, Robert Locke. I just wanted to be Daddy's little girl.

Love you, Daddy

Poetically Speaking

Mommy - 1/13/1992

A year ago today,

My beloved Mommy passed away,

Leaving behind,

Much joyous and painful memories,

Thoughts in my mind,

Which I could never let be,

Mommy's tender kisses,

Mommy's laughter,

I will never forget her,

From here on after,

Mommy's beautiful smile,

Which made life worthwhile,

Her beautiful sway,

That made men look her way,

And I will never forget,

She was loving and compassionate.

LaTarsia "Targie" Taylor

The Feeling You Give Me - 1/17/1992

Just the way you stare at me,
Sets my soul on fire,
I really care for you,
You're my heart and soul's desire,

I wouldn't want to dis you,
Because that would be unfair,
I hope you feel the same way,
At least have a little feeling there,

The way you call my name,
In a whisper I should say,
Makes my temperature rise,
In a very special way,

I want you so bad,
I would never want to upset you,
Because I would be
Depressed, down, out and blue.

I Won't Hurt You - 1/1992

I would never want to hurt you,

Or make you weep,

Because the love I have for you,

Is far too steep,

I hate when you say,

"Targie just don't dis me,"

Because I will never,

Your love is too sweet,

When you show that you care,

I will try my best to please you,

I would never try to hurt you,

Because my love is truly true.

LaTarsia "Targie" Taylor

<u>Wanting You - 1/1992</u>

Looking at you from a distance,
Or even up close,
I notice good things about you,
Your smile the most,
Your smile is charming,
Very distinctive I must say,
Your eyes have a glow,
Like diamonds in a way,
Your walk is manly,
Yet so smooth,
The more I watch,
The more I want you,
You keep your mustache
Trimmed and neat,
Even your lips
Look tasty and sweet,
Your skin is like silk,
It seems ever so right,
What would I give?
To have you for one night,
Maybe this is infatuation,
And it will soon pass,
Dang, how long
will me wanting you last?

Life Without You - 1/17/1992

Life without you,

Will have no meaning,

My life would be blue,

And my eyes pleading,

To have you back by my side,

To help me when I'm down,

And to wipe my tears when I cry,

Life without you,

Will have no cause,

There's no you in the future,

To hold anymore,

Life without you,

Will bring down my self-esteem,

You won't be there to fulfill my dreams.

LaTarsia "Targie" Taylor

<u>I Feel Trapped - 1/27/1992</u>

I can't do anything,
Yet you do everything,
You go where you want to go,
But when I want to, you say no,

I do love you,
And I would give you the world,
But if being your prisoner,
Means being your girl,
Then I'd rather be a diamond,
Instead of a pearl,

At least a diamond shines
Whether you like it or not,
But being a pearl,
I can roll, but with a touch,
I will stop,

I feel trapped,
And I want to be free,
But I can't if you make
A prisoner out of me.

Guilty – 1/27/1992

Somehow I feel guilty,

It's something I can't explain,

Somehow I feel trapped,

In one of these love games,

I put myself in a position

Which is hard to escape,

I should've thought sooner,

But now it's too late,

I've fallen in love,

With another girl's man,

Lord give me strength,

To let go and still stand.

LaTarsia "Targie" Taylor

Do What You Want - 1/27/1992

It always seems like you have fun,
I see the clouds and you see the sun,

Can't you see how I'm feeling inside?
Or do the tears have to pour from my eyes?

It seems like there's something else missing,
I get enough of your hugging and kissing,

But somehow my heart feels left out,
I know I'm sharing your love without a doubt.

♦♥♦

This is a lesson learned so take care of your business at home, that way your loved ones don't stray. I was still in love with my first, but I fell hard for my friend who had a girl. Obviously both of us were not getting enough attention at home so we experimented. I guess what our partners weren't giving us we gave to each other. Sometimes we take things for granted. Sometimes we think lust is love.

Poetically Speaking

Do You Still Love Her? - 1/27/1992

*Do you still love her,
Like you said you did?
Or did your love,
Slowly lose its grip?*

*I'm at the end
Of the rope now,
My feelings have changed,
And I don't know how,*

*I don't want to be
Number two anymore,
I want you for myself,
So I can score,*

*Do you still love her?
Because if you do,
I will lose interest,
And slip away from you.*

♦♥♦

That is exactly what I did. I left him alone and stayed with the dog I had. Of course I went back to dating others, but they claimed I was the only one. Whatever! At this point I didn't trust anybody with my heart. So these poems were for a couple of people in my life. Heck, some of them received the same exact poems at the same dang on time. Blame it on the game.

LaTarsia "Targie" Taylor

<u>Tomorrow - 1/27/1992</u>

The sun will come out tomorrow,

But not for me,

The good times pass me by,

Leaving pain and misery.

The sun will come out tomorrow,

Nope it was the rain,

Bringing more heartaches,

I am going insane.

The sun will come out tomorrow,

But I won't let it pass me by.

I will walk tall, stand proud,

And smile when I want to cry.

♦♥♦

That is crazy I wrote those previous 4 poems in one day. This one was written during second period in class. I guess I was so confused and mixed up that all I could do was write.

Kiss Off Or Shape Up - 2/13/1992

Some days you act like you don't want anything to do with me,
We hardly communicate do you love me or just my body?

You just want to see me, because you miss our sex,
But after you're satisfied what comes next?

Is it rejection until you're ready to bust a nut?
Come on I'm your girl, but I feel like your slut,

You must treat me as you want to be treated,
Because I will be a witch, trifling and conceited,

I won't cry no, I won't shed a tear,
So leave me alone or act like you care.

LaTarsia "Targie" Taylor

Thank You – 2/18/1992

Thank you for lending me a hand,

Now I know where I stand,

You know that commercial,

"A call can make your day,"

Well you made mine in every way,

Thank you for giving me

A shoulder to lean on,

Without your help,

I wouldn't be this strong,

I'll send this poem,

With just one demand,

Don't ever change,

Because you are a real man.

Hold Me Tight – 2/1992

Hold me, please don't let go,

Give me your love,

Spoil me, tell me

It's only me you're thinking of,

Don't let go of me,

Just don't hurt my heart,

You've spoiled me so far,

So why stop?

Hold me,

As if there was no tomorrow,

Don't let me go,

Because you'll leave me in sorrow.

LaTarsia "Targie" Taylor

<u>Diarrhea Blues - 2/1992</u>

Sitting on the toilet most of the day,
I have diarrhea, what else can I say,

It comes gushing out like water,
And it has a stinking smell,
My boyfriend is in the room,
But oh what the hell,

Everybody gets diarrhea once in a while,
So stop turning your face up and smile,

This is not as gross as it seems,
Well once the smell hits you,
You might turn green,
you know what I mean.

♦♥♦

Don't ask! I don't know what possessed me to write about this, but hey maybe somebody might not feel alone. Hell, I don't know.

Taking Time - 3/7/1992

Just thinking about you makes me blush,

Is this true love, or blind rebound lust?

We'll take our time to explore each other,

Our needs and wants,

We'll get to be mature lovers,

As time goes by,

That way our bond will be stronger,

And the scene would be right,

Just you just me,

Soon time will tell,

If we were meant to be,

Our friendship would prevail.

LaTarsia "Targie" Taylor

I'm Losing It – 3/18/1992

I'm losing it, really losing it,

I almost fell this morning,

And I stepped in dog dip,

I was late for school,

I left my coat in class too,

My stomach's been hurting,

And I'm feeling blue,

I've lost it,

Oh boy yes I have,

One minute I'm smiling,

The next I'm sad.

About "I'm Losing It"

Sometime in March my father came to get me. My cousin had supposedly told him that I was messing up. He said she called him and told him that I couldn't stay with her anymore, because I was hanging out with drug dealers and that I had dropped out of school. Mind you, I was going to high school. I had enrolled myself in night school to make up two classes so that I could graduate in June. Anyway life goes on. I moved to Maryland with my father unwillingly. If I was thinking it was only one month before my 18th birthday. I could have ran away and saved myself a lot of drama.

LaTarsia "Targie" Taylor

<u>*Mother's Day Is On Its Way - 5/8/1992*</u>

Mother's Day is coming, what am I going to do?
Mother's Day is coming, and I want to be with you,

Mother's Day is special, meant for you and me,
But you are in Heaven and I am on the streets,

Mother's Day is on its way, oh how will I smile?
If only I can visit Heaven and see you for a while,

For Mother's Day I will sit and think of you,
I will remember the fun things you use to do.

Poetically Speaking

So You Want To Live In This Garden – 5/1992

In my beautiful garden
Everyone is like me,
Some of us are different colors,
But the same internally,

In my waterbed
I can feel the rain when it comes,
Steady beating and pounding
Upon my beautiful garden,

Like the sun going up
We all rise,
Growing and growing,
And to my surprise,
We start disappearing,
What can it be?

Never judge a book by its cover, it isn't what it seems.
Now do you still want to live in this garden like me?

LaTarsia "Targie" Taylor

<u>Valley Flower Bed - 5/31/1992</u>

In a vast world of ongoing grief,
There stands one lonely rose,
The buds have fallen rapidly flowing
On and on with no place to go,

So lovely, yet fragile,
Silent as day & night,
This lonely rose,
Snatched away from earth itself,

Inside its screaming "Take me home"
But yet so mute,
No one hears its cries,
"Take me home to my family"
More budded roses,
Roses just like me.

♦♥♦

Well, I did finally leave in July and went to live with my first carnal love in Brooklyn, New York. Why did I do that? Another roller coaster ride of my life will take place.

In Love - 12/14/1992

Holding, hugging,

Missing, wanting,

and loving you too,

some of the things

that I only want to

do with you,

love has finally,

found me,

and I think it's true,

I hope you love me,

As much as I love you.

♦♥♦

Oh well, that didn't last long. I was back on the streets again. I went to live with my best friend Dana at that time. She was there for me through the worst moments in my life. Especially in 1990 when I had come to what I thought was the end of my rope. Wow! Only God has brought me through the storm. I wish I would have obeyed God sooner. I could have been saved from a lot of rough roads!

LaTarsia "Targie" Taylor

A Young Girl - 2/22/1993

A young girl,
Alone in the world,
No shoulder to lean on,
Just rocks and stones,

A young girl,
So fragile yet so alone,
Just three words I love you,
Will turn her gray skies blue,
Not even a dog or cat,
To talk to,

A young girl,
Alone in a world of fear,
People pass her by,
The hell if they care,
Another heart broken,
But into three,
No one to help her
Pain & misery,
No one to say,
I'll walk with thee.

A New Day - 2/22/1993

The sun is rising,
My temperature too,
I'm feeling lonely,
Heartbroken, and blue,
Now that you're gone,
I'm so confused,

The night has fallen,
The tears roll down,
I hear you calling,
Off goes my frown,

But I won't fall,
For your lies anymore,
My feelings,
Have ran out the door,
I will not tolerate
Any abuse,
To try our love again,
What's the use?

LaTarsia "Targie" Taylor

What Does It Take? - 2/1993

What does it take

For you to understand me?

I try to listen,

I try to explain,

But as always,

Misery is gained,

What does it take?

For you to respect me,

Please realize the things I want,

The experiences I've been through,

Most of all my love

Slowly slipping away from you,

One day you'll wake up

And I'll be gone yes free,

Because that's what it will take,

For you to appreciate me.

My Love For You - 3/9/1993

It's hard to express myself
After I've been hurt so many times,
It's hard to trust someone,
Especially with my hurt on the line,

I have friends yes indeed,
You are all the man I need,
My feelings for you,
Are strong and true,
Why would I lie to you?

I would never break your heart,
Or play games with your mind,
I'm a very special person,
And you are one of a kind.

♦♥♦

Remember my emotions were played with and I started playing the game too. So this was dedicated to someone I did care about, but since *"I love you,"* was used so loosely in my life I felt that everybody sometimes played the fool and it wasn't going to be me. In this era of my life some of the same poems were given to different guys.

LaTarsia "Targie" Taylor

The Story Of Love - 8/20/1993

Love without a season,
A body without a soul,
A year without seasons,
Something beyond control,

Respect lost along the line,
Trust has lost its way too,
Only darkness now you're blind,
A love once strong and true,

Arguments from here on,
Pain & misery a heavy load,
One minute here, now gone,
The story of love remains untold.

♦♥♦

I went back to Maryland, but this time I stayed with my Uncle Derek and Meachie. I was trying to run away from my problems and issues, but of course you can't run you must deal with every situation accordingly. This poem was dedicated to them.

Poetically Speaking

Love From A Distance – 9/26/1994

We may be separated by miles,
But it is the closeness in our hearts
That is keeping us together,
We have shared more than our bodies,
And true love last forever,

For distance may stand in the way now,
But when I close my eyes I see your smile,
When I lay down to sleep,
It is you in my sweet dreams,

So don't ever doubt my love,
Just let it be,
Because my feelings for you,
Are deep as the sea!

♦♥♦

A lot of stuff has happened. I ended up back in Brooklyn, New York. There are additional journals missing between now and 1996. I did find a few poems around that time frame.

LaTarsia "Targie" Taylor

Don't Hurt Me – 1996

Please don't hurt me I am only a child,
This attitude will only last a little while,
Open your arms for a great big hug,
I am only a child yearning to be loved,
No matter how far I make it in this world,
I will always remain your little girl,

The tears in my eyes,
The pain in my heart,
The shiver in my walk,
The pressure has to stop,
The betrayal of friends,
The unfaithful men,
What kind of world
Was I brought up in?

♦♥♦

My father's side was hurt, because I wouldn't stay in Maryland, but I was too damaged and blind to the love that they were trying to show me. Well at least some of them, because there were some judgmental people that would make the worst in me come to the surface, but that is another story. I love my father even though my Mommy raised me. He tried to save me after my teen years got the best of me, but I was not in the mood to be saved and anyhow he had his own stuff to deal with. Some of my paternal family did try to save me and I thank them for that. They know who they are.

Lovers In '96 Are In A Deep Ship

Love has no name,
It's all a game,
A four letter word,
Without a cause,
But yet it's something
We all long for,
I love you baby
I hear you say,
Yet someone comes along
And you're cheating anyway,
So you loved him last night
And hate him today,
Love, love, love,
Take me away,
To where?
I don't know,
To where the birds fly,
And the green grass grows,
Take me to the ocean,
So I can see,
The fish swimming so gracefully,
Altogether in the deep sea,
Slowly, swiftly, suddenly,
They are multiplying in the deep sea.

LaTarsia "Targie" Taylor

Pure Bitterness – 1996

Bitterness overcomes my peace of mind,

Evilness overcomes the love I have inside,

Happiness has left my heart a long time ago,

Envy, hate, and jealousy fills my soul,

This new woman has changed the game,

No longer will I ever be the same,

What's wrong with me? Why can't I cry?

My life is wrong, who can make it right?

I have to survive this crazy damn life.

If I don't fight then surely I will die.

A Made up Mind – 1996

This is interesting and somehow deep,
I just seen "Waiting to Exhale" and I feel free,
I'm going to further my education,
And be the woman that I am meant to be,
Because if I depend on a man
I would surely lose my mind,
Most of them are cheaters,
And liars of all kinds,
They are unfaithful to the bone,
That's why I have one away,
And one at home,
You can say I'm never satisfied,
Because what one won't do,
The other will supply,
I am a woman with many needs,
As I satisfy you, you must satisfy me,
Being the controller,
That's what I am,
I am strong willed,
And your heart I will win.

LaTarsia "Targie" Taylor

An Angel in Disguise – 12/22/1996

Thank you for taking time to let me speak,
Usually when I talk no one listens to me,
Thank you for caring when others gave up,
You are truly an Angel from Heaven above,

Thank you for smiling back,
There's nothing like a smile returned for the day,
Because through all the chaos,
You always remember that one smiling face,

You are faithful in all the things you do,
And I hope people return that joy unto you,
I knew Heaven was missing an Angel,
For a while too,
But I found that Angel,
because God put that Angel in you.

Poetically Speaking

♦♥♦

About "An Angel in Disguise"

Wow! Just when I thought there wasn't any other way, Janet Hoyte led me back to church. I became a member of The Cathedral of Christ Community Ministries in 1996. God, once again became the love of my life. Of course I had to shed all of the habits that I picked up in the world, but hey it was a start. Now don't get me wrong, my Mommy did raise us in the church and others tried along the way especially Bishop, the Godfather of my first carnal love but, I chose another path. I was led astray. Thanks to my first carnal love because without him I would not have met you. I thank God for you. You have a golden heart, and have always made me laugh when I was feeling blue. I remember having choir rehearsal with the whole crew. Jay, I really love you.

♦♥♦

LaTarsia "Targie" Taylor

Love Lets You Feel - 11/11/1997

They say I'm crazy,
But I think not,
I feel the pain of a crying baby,
The stress of the homeless in a lot,
I feel the woe of an alcoholic,
And the drama of a drug addict,
Insanity is what they call it,
But a gift is what I predict,
I may not be a magician,
And I may not be God,
But the cure for all is within,
For everyone has love in their heart,
And when you seek it,
You shall find it,
Love deep, love strong,
God's love will help you carry on.

Scripture Reference(s)

Hebrews 13:1 - 3 · 1 Thessalonians 4:8 - 10

Poetically Speaking

Only The Strong Survive - 11/25/1997

On the verge of giving up,
But yet some strong will is holding on,
My life seems dead,
But yet I'm still living,
Lord I'm asking,
Just where do I belong?
I've cried and cried,
I've loved and loved,
But no matter how hard I try,
It seems like my all isn't enough,
They say a penny for your thoughts,
But mine ain't worth a dime,
Maybe it's me,
O ye of little faith,
In a world where only the strong survive,
Lord I believe in myself,
Most of all I believe in you,
Lord give me strength,
To make it in this world,
A world so cold and blue.

Scripture Reference(s)

Jeremiah 31:3 - 34 · Luke 12:28 - 29

LaTarsia "Targie" Taylor

Missing You Mommy - 11/27/1997

As I look around me,
I see you everywhere I turn,
Your beautiful eyes,
Your smile,
And all the beauty you possess,
I see you holding me,
When I was a child,
I see you everywhere Mommy,
I've been missing you for a while,
I miss saying Mommy,
And listening to you,
I love you Mommy,
And I am missing you too,
I would give anything
Just to have you back,
But I guess that's impossible,
Until I meet with you,
At the end of my road.
Where the streets are paved with gold.

Scripture Reference(s)

Isaiah 61:3

Poetically Speaking

<u>The Strength In Our Life - 12/1998</u>

God is the joy and strength in our life,
Yes God will and He can make it all right,
Our Creator, Doctor, Lawyer, and Friend,
Yes God will guide us until the very end,

Times are tough and it seems like no one cares,
Just call out to Jesus and he will be right there,
You have to call on him, he won't force you,
God loves us so much that He gave us free will,

So please pick your head up, wipe your tears away,
Believe, have faith and the Holy Spirit will guide your way,
Yes you fell down and you are feeling ashamed,
It's human to err so repent and praise his name,

You've been wanting or needing a job, house or car,
Look to Jesus he's your light when times are dark.

<u>Scripture Reference(s)</u>

1 Kings 8:47 · Romans 8

LaTarsia "Targie" Taylor

Dear Grandma & Grandpa: I've Learned - 12/1998

Thank you for caring, thank you for bearing all of my hardships,
I know I am not the easiest grandchild to bear,
But I do know that I've learned from my mistakes,
I have learned to be grateful for the things that I do have,
I've learned to take the bitter with the sweet,
I've learned how to listen and not to speak,
Instead of jumping up and saying this is the way I want to do it,
So I will do it this way,
I learned that being hard headed will ruin the path I have to take,
It's not what I've been through, but what I have learned,
I have learned that obedience is very important,
I have learned that your love for me is great,
Because out of all the negative things I've done,
You have never cut me off or abandoned me,
I want to thank you for your patience,
Thank you for being my backbone when I was weak,
Thank you most of all for being yourselves,
I love you dearly and words can't express how I really feel,
So don't ever change, you are special and real.

Poetically Speaking

A Lesson Learned - 12/1998

I'm here to tell a story it's up to you to listen and learn,
Wisdom does not come easy just live and it will be earned,
Not too long ago in the world I was filthy and unclean,
If you've ever been blind then you know what I mean,
Not living for today,
Worried about tomorrow, and dwelling on yesterday,
And in the darkness believe me, there's only hell to pay,
I was somewhere in a zone, in my mind I felt so alone,
I was trying to please flesh and blood,
But flesh and blood wasn't pleasing me,
Living like this can cause your spiritual,
Mental and physical health to decrease,
I was a prisoner of my own ignorance, but I wanted to be free,
I called on Jesus and he came down and anointed me,
I found out that God was, is and will always be my grace,
Now I'm not ashamed to look the righteous in their face,
I was deaf, God's words of wisdom I didn't want to hear,
Now I can hear joyful sounds flowing through my ears,
When you hear me singing and I start to cry,
Don't you fear, God is blessing me by and by,
I sing because I know what this world can do,
If you don't believe in God then you are through,
I thank you Lord for a new mind, walk, and talk,
I thank you for restoring my faith and everything, for now I
know the reason why I sing.

LaTarsia "Targie" Taylor

Rest In Peace Chico – 1/4/1999

I have searched within my heart to express how I feel,
I can't explain but in all ways he had that whip appeal,
He was smooth and a heartbreaker I must say,
But still something about him just made your day,
He had a good personality and always made you laugh,
Through good and bad times he was a true friend to have,
Somehow when he was wrong he would make it seem right,
If you had a problem he would be there day or night,
If you were hungry he would fill your tummy,
If you were sad he'd say something funny,

He wasn't perfect we all have our own funny moods,
But I do know if push came to shove he'd be there for you,
He was charming the kind of man most women desired,
Just his very presence sets your soul on fire,
When he walked in the room I would start to blush,
Or in situations he would hold my hand and I would get a rush,
Finally Chico I have to say I love you and I truly do,
It would be hard to replace another friend like you,
Without you I'll try to be strong because I know you are free,
So sleep our dearly beloved, sleep in Heavenly peace.

Poetically Speaking

♦♥♦

About "Rest In Peace Chico"

This poem was about one of my friends from public school. We tried the dating thing after the drama our loves put us through, but it didn't work out, and we both decided to remain friends.

♦♥♦

LaTarsia "Targie" Taylor

The Devil Thought He Had Me – 2/7/1999

I don't know where I'm going,

But I can tell you where I've been,

And life without God,

Leads to death deep within,

The devil had me for a while,

But now he has to let me be,

I called on God,

Because I'm his child,

And God has set me free,

So now in my heart,

Where it was empty,

I now have joy

And God's inner peace!

Scripture Reference(s)

Isaiah 55

Poetically Speaking

Waiting For My Wedding Night - 2/10/1999

You say my eyes are dark brown,

But my heart says they are blue,

For my tears are like a waterfall,

Continually flowing water for you,

Where are you the love of my life?

I just don't understand,

I am supposed to be someone's wife,

For God said to be fruitful and multiply,

But I haven't had a chance,

I guess only God knows,

When I'll have my wedding dance, I guess

When the time is right,

So I'll try to wait patiently, and prepare myself

For my wedding night.

LaTarsia "Targie" Taylor

Your Kiss – 5/1999

When we met I knew from the start,

With just one kiss you'd capture my heart,

The first date I was strong I kept my distance,

On the second date you were hard to resist,

A good night hug, a kiss good bye,

Gosh your lips were juicy oh my, my, my,

I knew you felt me as I felt you,

Because my knees buckled and yours did too,

As your tongue went in my mouth,

I let you lead, and got wet down south,

When you kissed me I was on cloud nine,

Not to mention the jitterbugs in my spine,

Boy oh boy I can't wait to see you again,

Maybe next time I'll get goose bumps on my skin.

It's Over Before It Begins – 1999

I want to know, before I let go,

I don't know what to say,

Or where to start this poem,

But things aren't the same,

Since I came home,

Our conversations are shorter,

And we are stalling for things to say,

We are both holding back something

That's in the way,

Maybe you don't want a commitment,

But we can have an open relationship,

If last weekend caused a lot of chaos,

Then I apologize,

I'm sorry, but I have a lot bottled inside,

I hope in the future things will change,

If not then screw it, I tried anyway.

LaTarsia "Targie" Taylor

Okay Leave Me Alone - 6/1999

When will you listen?
When will you learn?
Why can't you see?
Playing with fire you will get burned,
You say "What's there to lose?"
Honey just look around you,
There are others who yearn
To be in your shoes,
Why does it have to be this way?
I know life is a game,
But you don't have to play,
No, Honey not this way,
If only you would stop and think,
About the life you're living,
Honey you are not alone,
Everybody has their wants and needs,
But you want it all,
And it doesn't come easy,
We all have a ladder to climb,
So leave me alone,
And let me live my life.

Poetically Speaking

Enough Backsliding – 6/2/1999

Lord please forgive my actions,
My trespasses, yes my sins,
Lord I'm stumbling,
But I want to make it in,

Lord I need you in my life,
To hold me up high,
Because without you,
I would not be alive,

Lord I do love you,
Please have mercy,
Lord protect, and comfort me,

Especially in times like this,
When I turn and start to slip,
I need you more
Than this world has to give.

Scripture Reference(s)

Hosea 14:4
"I will heal their backsliding, I will love them freely: for mine anger is turned away from him."

LaTarsia "Targie" Taylor

Disappointment - 8/21/1999

I have struggled, I have been here and there,

You want my trust, but hell, why should I care,

With me it doesn't matter if I win or lose,

At least I am no longer depending on you,

There is nothing like being let down by a friend,

Shoot, they are suppose to be there until the end,

You keep saying trust me, but why should I?

Where were you, when the tears took a ride,

When I needed a warm shoulder to cry on,

Or somebody to make me laugh in my storm?

Huh, no answer so I'll say this again,

I stick with myself,

Because I'll love me until the end,

Just me, myself, and I,

Yes they are my best friends.

Poetically Speaking

Who Is God? - 8/21/1999

I see people praying,
But to who?
Is God real?
Can God love you?
Can God Heal?

I am waiting for an answer,
But I get no reply,
I look to Heaven,
But is God in the sky?

Is God inside of me?
They say the Holy Spirit is,
Can I rely on him?
I guess I'll wait and see,
Yes I will wait for victory.

Scripture Reference(s)

Genesis 1 · Genesis 28:13 · Exodus 3:14
Exodus 15:26 · John 3:16 · John 5:19 - 27 · Acts 2

LaTarsia "Targie" Taylor

<u>Suppression - 8/21/1999</u>

I have a lot to say,

But I hold it inside,

I want to do so much,

But I hold back, why?

Am I afraid of failure?

Is this worth my while?

Can what I think hurt me,

Or will it make me smile?

I want to let it go,

But the fear of rejection

Keeps it suppressed,

I want to let go of the fear,

And put my mind to the test.

Poetically Speaking

<u>I Don't Want To Rush - 8/26/1999</u>

When you look into my eyes,
It's like mental telepathy,
I have to turn away,
Because you're slowly undressing me,

I don't want to rush it,
I want to take it nice and slow,
Maintaining our friendship,
Then let our love flow.

Best things come to those who wait,
With love it is a give or take,
I can't afford to lose,
Not with my heart at stake,

So let's ride this thing out,
Until the end of the road
Because like I always say,
The story of love remains untold.

LaTarsia "Targie" Taylor

Our Relationship – 9/9/1999

I look into your eyes and I see the truth,

In many ways you're as honest as I am to you,

But of course there will be temptation thrown our way,

It will be up to us to be strong and stand in the evil day,

First we can communicate and that's the key,

Second of all have trust, respect, and honesty,

With all of the above we'll understand each other,

Time will go by and we'll be inseparable lovers.

Poetically Speaking

The Rhythm Of Music - 1999

The rhythm of music,

Sometimes smooth as can be,

The rhythm of music,

Rolling & racing with the sea,

Slow jams playing on and on,

Like a bird humming a song,

Fast, free, foreshadowed by you,

Music has rhythm & meaning too,

Drums, guitars, pianos,

What else is there?

The sweet sound of instruments,

Moving through the air,

It is only the melody,

The rhythm of music,

Is good to hear,

Beautiful notes

Flowing way up there.

LaTarsia "Targie" Taylor

Let Me In – 1999

If only I could understand you,

But you won't let me,

If only I could touch you,

Converse with you mentally,

But you have put up a road block,

And I can't reach you,

Open up don't be resistant,

I'll show you a love that's true,

They say the eyes tell a story,

But you won't let me read yours,

Just believe in me take a risk,

Open up to my love at your door,

With the good times there's always bad,

But that doesn't mean to dwell on the past,

I want to love you,

And for you to love me the same,

But like a pair of jeans,

Eventually my love will fade away.

Poetically Speaking

<u>Forget About It - 9/1999</u>

I know with you I had the most satisfying sex,

But it's over there's a reason you're my ex,

I still haven't forgotten the crap you put me through,

Forgiven you, I have, but I won't go back with you.

Yes I know that I loved you, but things have changed,

I'm more of a woman and my standards aren't the same,

So stop saying sorry and begging for another chance,

I have awakened, now I am no longer under your trance.

The thrill is gone, like these old songs

So keep on moving, change is gonna come

You thought I'd seen the rain, but I have seen the sun

So step off because girls just wanna have fun.

LaTarsia "Targie" Taylor

<u>Stay Strong – 1999</u>

Sometimes the road gets tough,

But just keep on trying,

We all have times that are rough,

and we feel like dying,

You can't let your problems

Hold you down,

Raise your head up high

And turn that frown around,

This world is full of trials

& tribulations,

But trust in God and he will

Fix any situation.

<u>Scripture Reference(s)</u>

Isaiah 40:28 - 31 · Ezra: 9:6 - 15

How Can I Love You? - 3/22/2000

Where did the feelings come from?
Please help me understand,

One minute I'm rejecting you,
Then I want you for my man,

How can love fit in?
When I don't want it,

How can you love someone?
Who is not ready to commit,

What am I suppose to do?
Now that you are here,

Loving you too much,
Is something I can't bear!

LaTarsia "Targie" Taylor

<u>Wait on the Lord – 6/8/2000</u>

Lord I'm slipping
I have fallen astray,
I know I can't make it
Without any faith,

So Lord I'm asking for
More strength today,
I need you to guide me
The straight and narrow way,

Yes Lord I will be still
Yes Lord for you I'll wait,
Because I want to live
And enter Heaven's gate,

If it means a year
Or more at stake,
Then I will,
I will truly wait.

<u>Scripture Reference(s)</u>

Psalm 27

Poetically Speaking

Why? Why? Why? – 6/8/2000

Why should I cry?
Why should I shed a tear?
When you are most high
God you can cure
All of my fears,
Why should I be afraid?
Why should I ever doubt?
When you give me life
With much love to sprout,
Why should I be discouraged?
Why am I ashamed?
When I can be encouraged
And call on Jesus' name,

Lord I will close my eyes,
Lord I will walk in faith,
Lord I will stop asking why,
You have shown me the way,
Lord thank you for everything,
The good times and the bad,
Lord for you I will sing,
For your love is the most
Ultimate love I've ever had.

Scripture Reference(s)

Psalm 23

LaTarsia "Targie" Taylor

Who Do You Think You Are? - 6/8/2000

How can you judge me?
When you don't know the half,
You look at my appearance,
Then you whisper and laugh,
Well my clothes may not be expensive,
But they sure are clean,
And because I look weak or sensitive,
Doesn't give you a right to be mean,
I want to know who in the world
Do you think you are?
Honey when I get to Heaven,
I can't bring clothes or cars,
I will go as I came naked,
Naked as the stars,
"What good is a man
If he gains the world
And loses his soul?
Honey read the bible,
Learn of stories untold.

Scripture References

Matthew 16:25 - 28 · Proverbs 28:25 - 28

Poetically Speaking

A Sinner's Prayer & My Guess on God's Response – 6/8/2000

ME:
Lord I am sick and my body is weak,
I don't understand why this is happening to me,
I do say my prayers and I try to be nice,
Okay sometimes I pray in my bed at night,
I go to church on Easter, Christmas, and now & then,
So Lord why can't you forgive all of my sins?
Oh Lord I do thank you for money and a man too,
But I ask you questions and I don't hear from you.
GOD:
You say you are sick and your body is weak,
I spoke of healing, yet you do not believe,
You say your prayers, but only at night,
For two minutes or less, where is my time?
There were some days you were nice,
But you did a lot of bad things on spite,
I am merciful and forgiving too,
You don't forgive, so why should I forgive you?
"Money," where I am you can't bring it with you,
And yes I give you friends "Not men to screw,"
O Foolish Galatians, who hath bewitched you?
Your sins can be forgiven, but you must repent,
I do love you child despite your stubbornness,
In spite of your hard head, and rebellion too,
Your sins can be forgiven, repent and be faithful,
I am your FATHER and I LOVE YOU.

LaTarsia "Targie" Taylor

All Alone – 9/26/2000

Sitting here on the verge of tears,
Now it's over after all these years,

If only I would have seen the signs,
Isn't that the truth "love is blind"?

How can you leave me without a clue?
I dedicated my heart and soul to you,

I fell in love and forgot the rules,
Never let love turn you into a fool,

You broke my heart, but it's all right,
I will get up, walk proud and shine,

Thank you Honey for a lesson learned,
If you play with fire you will get burned.

Poetically Speaking

Count Your Blessings – 1/10/2001

Don't forget to count your blessings,
When your burdens are tying you down,

Don't forget to count your blessings,
God will turn your whole life around,

Praise him regardless of what may be,
Thank him in advance for everything,

I won't forget to count my blessings,
I will thank God who reigns in Heaven.

Scripture Reference(s)

Psalm 34

"I will bless the Lord at all times: his praises shall continually be in my mouth.
My soul shall make her boast in the Lord: the humble shall hear thereof, and be glad.
O magnify the Lord with me, and let us exalt his name together."

LaTarsia "Targie" Taylor

I Am Longing – 6/14/2001

I am longing,

For someone to hold me,

I am longing,

For someone to mold me,

I am longing,

For a love strong and true,

I am longing,

Can I be fulfilled by you?

Then be a man and step up to the plate,

Let's join hand in hand for goodness sake,

If not then we can go our separate ways,

It is better to split than to suffer and stay.

Poetically Speaking

♦♥♦

About "*I Am Longing*"

Here I go again with love. Nobody wins. What was I thinking? You would think I would stay in the game being a player, but no I wanted to settle down again and try love one more time. I think someone should have taken a bucket of ice and thrown it on me. It would have awakened me. I would have smelled the coffee. It just wasn't my time. Whew, the emotions we allow ourselves to go through just to please the flesh. Goodness, gracious, when is enough - enough? Behind my wall I guess I wasn't that tough.

If we put all our time and energy into God rather than humans, life would be very pleasant and easier. We are unforgiving towards our family members & friends holding onto some grudges for years, but our mates can hurt us much more than they did, and we would forgive our lovers faster than John Doe can mow the lawn. They say that "Blood is thicker than water," but I learned that "Semen is thicker than blood." So if the above happens to you, please remember what I said, and shake the dust off of your feet and be careful who *lies* in your bed.

♦♥♦

LaTarsia "Targie" Taylor

Mirror Image – 7/1/2001

I was minding my own business and to my surprise,
I saw this disturbing image on the opposite side,
This girl looked so pitiful, she had issues indeed,
She sure was lost; no way would this ever be me,

An emptiness was in her eyes, oh yes I do recall,
Her eyes were red, puffy and discolored too,
Her eyes carried a burden, oh boy isn't life cruel,

"Thou shall not judge, lest ye be judged"
Passed through my mind,
So instead of being skeptical,
I decided to be kind,
I said hello, but there was no reply,
I told her it's better to give it to God,
Than to hold it inside,

Still no response, so I reached out to touch her,
Oh no, this cannot be, my world is a sudden blur,
For this was an image of me,

When looking on the outside we see the physical,
Being judgmental, so for love we leave no room,
We are quick to tell someone else what to do,
But who are we to judge?
When we aren't walking in their shoes,

I was quick to tell her to get on her knees,
But did I do that
When I found out it was an image of me?

Mirror Image - 7/1/2001 - (continued)

This is a sad case of do as I say, not as I do,
So before you think about judging me,
Stop and take a real good look at you,

Some people have pebbles to carry,
While others have stones,
We don't know all the reasons,
Why someone's heart is cold,

So if you happen to see someone in need,
And they don't talk to you,
Just get on your knees and pray to God,
A simple prayer will do,
Or just touch the mirror,
That person might be you.

Scripture Reference(s)

John 8

LaTarsia "Targie" Taylor

Be Still - 9/27/2001

Like a tree firmly planted
In fertile land,
With you Lord
I'll be strong,
Doing my best to stand,

Yes the evil darts
Are flying around me,
But I will try to be still
In times of adversity,

Lord you are my wing
That lets me soar above,
Nothing not anything
Can take away that love.

Scripture Reference

Isaiah 54:17

"No weapon that is formed against thee shall prosper; and every tongue that shall rise against thee in judgment thou shalt condemn. This is the heritage of the servants of the Lord, and their righteousness is of me, saith the Lord."

Poetically Speaking

<u>To Grandpa - 2/2002</u>

I would like to thank you Grandpa for being who you are,
There is so much to say I don't know where to start,

I guess I can tell you that I love you so,
Indeed you spoiled me and never told me no,

You had that stern look so you didn't have to yell at me,
When wrong, if looks could kill I would've been six foot deep,

I thank you grandpa for always listening,
Even though I talk too much,
I always knew when you wanted me to be quiet,
But you never said shut up,
You'd just nod your head and sometimes cough,

Of course I would keep on yacking,
Probably getting under your skin,
You are more than my grandpa,
You are my silent friend,

I thank God for blessing you through the years,
By His Grace you've made it through many toils and snares,

Well congratulations on your retirement, relax, and explore,
Again, I love you and may God bless you more and more.

LaTarsia "Targie" Taylor

Sometimes – 3/2002

Sometimes a hug is all we need,
You'll be surprised with the stress it relieves,

Sometimes a kiss will show you care,
And dry some of your inner and outer tears,

Sometimes a smile can heal spiritually,
Lifting you up physically or emotionally,

Sometimes a side talk will let you know,
People carry pebbles while others have stones,

Sometimes giving love turns gray skies blue,
So pray for others, because someone is praying for you.

Scripture Reference(s)

Psalm 34:19
"Many are the afflictions of the righteous: but the Lord delivereth him out of them all."

Job 33:26
"He shall pray unto God, and he will be favourable unto him: and he shall see his face with joy: for he will render unto man his righteousness."

Poetically Speaking

Lord I Need – 5/16/2002

I need joy Lord,
Unspeakable joy,
Flowing like a river,
I need understanding Lord,
So I won't be afraid,
I need faith Lord,
Like Moses at the Red Sea,
I need healing Lord,
Touch my body,
Yes healing Lord,
Please set me free,
I need discernment Lord,
Open up my eyes,
Let me not judge,
But be virtuous and wise,
Oh Lord I trust you,
And I love you too,
So I will stand strong,
And walk with you,
Through the pain,
The trials and rain,
I will hold on,
Yes I will stand strong.

Scripture Reference(s)

Proverbs 31:10 - 31
I want to be a virtuous woman.

LaTarsia "Targie" Taylor

When Care Is Pressing You Down - 5/16/2002

When care is pressing you down a bit,
And it seems like you can't take it,

Close your eyes and believe in God,
Concentrate on him, it is not hard,

Believe in yourself with all your might,
Loving yourself can make you right,

So don't ever doubt the love within you,
God will love, guide, and protect you too,

Just have faith and give God a chance,
And he will give you a new song and dance.

Scripture Reference(s)

Isaiah 45:5 - 8

Poetically Speaking

In Loving Memory of Hazel - 6/11/2002

A lady well known,
A lady well loved,
Who has been called,
To Heaven above,
The joy in her smile,
Makes you want to stay for a while,
She had her days,
Some good and bad too,
But we all have our up and down moods,
She took in children, after hers were raised,
To God in Heaven, She gave all her praise,
If she were here I'm sure she'd say,
Don't cry for me, because I'm okay,
I have walked this road,
Done carried this load,
So just listen and do what's told,
Be happy for me, because I am free,
No more pain, no more worries,
So don't you cry,
Stop wondering why,
She's with her Maker up in the sky,
So live your life to the fullest,
Because we are on borrowed time!

♦♥♦

This was dedicated to my friend Monique in loving memory of her Grandmother.

LaTarsia "Targie" Taylor

<u>Another Love, Let Go! – 7/26/2002</u>

You need someone who runs the streets like you,
So when you are outside she'll be out there too,
Obviously you are happy with the way things are,
But I'm not and my heart has enough damn scars,

What's keeping you here?
What's making you stay away?
I can't deal with you hanging out,
Only God knows where everyday,
Maybe we should part for a while,
For my tender heart has lost its smile,

Why should I be lonely when my man lives with me?
That's what I get for being trusting and living unholy,
I know one thing for sure, I am tired to the bone,
Being with you sucks, and I'd rather be left alone.

♦♥♦

I was finally living alone in Brooklyn for the first time in my life. God blessed me thanks to my Grandma and Grandpa. Of course, you know I messed up. After four months of living alone, I let my man move in from 2002-2006. We had our ups and downs. That's how this poem was written. After about two months of living together, this dude decided to run the streets and I was constantly arguing and fighting with him, yet I decided to stay. Four years of a roller coaster ride.

Poetically Speaking

I'll Go Through Lord – 7/28/2002

Oh my heart is troubled,
And my days are lonely,
But I'll hold unto God,
For it is God that holds me,

I will just sit still,
And wait on Him,
This might be a test,
That I am put in,

I'll go through Lord,
Yes I'll go through,
For men can't help,
This is spiritual,

My troubles will soon end,
Yes indeed,
I do believe,
Because Jesus is my friend,
He's my brother,
And Savior too,
Yes Lord yes,
With you I'll go through.

Scripture Reference(s)

Psalm 27

LaTarsia "Targie" Taylor

It's a Thin Line - 7/29/2002

You say you don't trust me,
Well I don't know what to do,
I have apologized,
Now it's up to you,
But think long and hard
About the stuff you put me through,
So consider us both wrong
For the things we do,
Where is your time?
Why can't I spend it with you?
Whatever! And you say our love is true,
I want things to change,
From this moment on,
Because you are losing me,
Hell, I'm almost gone,
Damn it! Wake up
Before it's too late,
Love me or move on,
Because this I can't take.

Poetically Speaking

<u>My Anger Has Set In - 7/30/2002</u>

Well let me tell you something about you,
First of all it's not screw me, but screw you,

You don't know about love, yet you say ours is true,
You try to play games, but I'm not your damn fool,

You said I was selfish when all I thought about was you,
So now let us switch places, you sit at home feeling blue,

Because my heart is tired and my mind is too,
You must be blind if you think forever I'll be with you,

I deserve better than this, nah man I am not with it,
So yes I will find someone else to spend my life with,

But for now screw you, it's over now, somehow,
You managed to flip my smile upside down,

But now my sadness is gone, and anger has set in,
So bounce fool, and find a new dumb & blind friend.

LaTarsia "Targie" Taylor

In Loving Memory Of Uncle Fitz - 7/2002

Where do I start, where do I begin?
Uncle Fitz was true, he was a friend,
Never judgmental always fair,
He sat back, but he still cared,
He was one to talk and let you be,
So you can look at yourself and see,
These roads in life are hard sometimes,
And a hard head makes a soft behind,
Some people leave footprints,
Some people leave scars,
But this man was Heaven sent,
Blessed, and saved by far,
He had an authority in his stand,
Gaining respect without demand,
Thank you Lord for this blessed Angel,
Who has shown his love,
Thank you Lord for this blessed Angel,
Who lies in Heaven above.

What's Going On? - 8/24/2002

You said I was demanding,
So I let you lead the way,
Now it seems as if you care
Less and less every day,

I don't know what's going on,
But I know what I see,
You are there for everyone,
Everyone except me,

A little time
Never hurt anyone,
Shoot, I'm seeing clouds
And you are laughing
In the sun.

Doing this and doing that,
Pursuing Mary and Mat,
When I am right here,
And this is where it's at.

LaTarsia "Targie" Taylor

Why So Much Pain? - 9/14/2002

What went wrong?
Where is the love?
Where is the respect?
Oh Lord is Heaven above?
We haven't finished yet,

My eyes have cried,
Pouring rivers of pain,
God I ask you why,
Must I go through this pain?

♦♥♦

Okay let me pause and go back for a minute. In February 1995, while I was living in Maryland I fell sick. The doctors diagnosed me with ulcerative colitis, and psoriasis of the skin. So from 1995 and thereafter, some of the pain and misery poems weren't over a man, they were because of my physical being. I was going on 22 years old and didn't accept these diseases. In 2002 I was also diagnosed with arthritis. To top it off, I was not taking my medication. I was supposed to be dead a couple of times due to the loss of blood, but God! Through the years as my faith grew, God was healing me. My intestines were severely damaged, but through the prayers of my family, church, and friends, God restored my stomach. Now a little scar remains on my left side. With faith, I know I will be 100% healed instead of 85%. This poem was written in my time of a flare up. Well, that's what the doctor's called it. During that time, I said, "I should write a book." Wow! God's grace and mercy has kept me. Thank you, Lord.

Poetically Speaking

<u>*In Loving Memory of My Step-Dad - 11/23/2002*</u>

In loving memory to a man well known,
Who has finished his journey,
Who has finally gone home,
From God's green earth,
Where time is short,
Where salvation is earned,
And surely not brought,
As I look to the sky,
Where the birds roam free,
I'll look to the Heavens,
For that's where you'll be,
I'll remember your smile,
Your gentle touch,
All the little things,
That mean so much,
Although today is full of sorrow,
Your memory will forever brighten tomorrow.

Written by: LaToya Taylor

LaTarsia "Targie" Taylor

Help Me Lord – 11/2002

Lord you know I have carried
This heavy load for far too long,
These ghosts are riding my back,
Get off and let me sing my song,

Lord I've done had my share of pain,
Take this cup and inside of me reign,
I need to let go so my light can shine,
Lord I know you are always on time,

I need to keep my mind on you God,
And stop worrying about life being hard,
You know I've had some ups and downs,
And only you God, you change my frown,

I will praise you in the midst of my pain,
I'm going to shout and praise your name,
All of my worries and bad habits too,
Lord you know all that I'm going through,

I have to stop putting my trust in man,
Flesh and blood is not the way,
Please help me to take a stand,
And have mercy if I fall astray.

Poetically Speaking

Dear God – 12/21/2002

Thank you for another day,
I don't know where to begin,
And I don't know what to say,
I'll start by thanking you for your grace and mercy,
Lord please forgive me,
I have fallen from the tree,
How can I go on living a lie?
How can I say I love you
When I'm sleeping with this guy?
I don't want to lose
The trust you have in me,
So dear God
I'm asking for you to set me free,
Show me the way to go
Which road shall I take?
Let your still voice
Lead me always,
Save those around me,
Including the one I love,
Show us how to live,
So we can make it above,
I want to live with you forever and a day,
Lord please save me, and show me the way.

Scripture Reference(s) – A Cry of Distress

Psalm 69

LaTarsia "Targie" Taylor

Ooh, Darkskin Brotha - 3/6/2003

Ooh, you are so fine,
Looking at you from way behind.
The arch in your back,
I like the way you move like that.
Standing there posing,
And observing the crowd
Ooh, I know you make every man's woman proud!
Turn around, and let me get a better look,
Um, um, um, tasty fine,
Sweet as can be.
What can I do to get you next to me?
Darkskin Brotha, what's your name?
Ooh, let me guess
It gotta be Jermaine,
Because you have those juicy lips,
And those slick eyebrows,
With that low haircut,
Shaped up to the "T".
What, what, what can I do to get you next to me?
Darkskin Brotha, you are sooooo fine,
But Darkskin Brotha, I can't make you mine.
You are a Darkskin Brotha too fine for me.

Written by: LeChema Taylor-McGuire

Just You, Just Me – 3/9/2003

I am just thinking of the time when we first met,
I was feeling you, but I was playing hard to get,
After you gave me your number I tried not to call,
Eventually I gave in, was it meant to be after all?
Your first visit to my house, remember that night?
We were hand in hand and it felt ever so right,
Along the way I found out you came with two,
So I accepted your child, because I cared for you,
On our road together we hurt each other so,
But trials and tribulations make us inseparable,
When we lost contact for those two years,
I searched and searched ending up in tears,
I never wanted to love again, I was through,
Eventually I tried to forget about knowing you,
As time passed I was working and keeping busy,
But as fate would have it you came back to me,
Although these two years have been trying,
I will hold on to you and keep on fighting,
We have come too far to turn back now,
We will make it some way and somehow,
I won't let you go as long as you hold on too,
Because you belong to me, and I belong to you.

LaTarsia "Targie" Taylor

With God - 4/2003

If all of my days were bright and sunny,
There would be no room for tears,
I would take life for granted,
Never ever having a care,

But because of my road,
I know of a Savior
Who can ease your pain,
Yes God can take away the rain,

I may be a dreamer,
But I know my joy draweth near,
I believe in Jesus Christ,
And I know God really cares,

So my faith stands strong,
I know He will comfort me,
My heart and soul has let God in,
For He is Almighty,
God is my Father until the end.

Scripture Reference(s)

Romans 5

Hold On – 4/1/2003

I'm going to hold on,
Through my ups and downs,
Yes I'll be holding on,
When that job has laid me off,
I will dust my feet and stand up,

Hold on
When trials come,
Too heavy to bear,
Hold on
Know that God
Is still right there,

Hold on
When the money is low,
And bills are due,
Hold on
God will see you through.

Scripture Reference(s)

Exodus 14:13 – 14 · John 14:1 - 4

LaTarsia "Targie" Taylor

Holding Up Your Hands - 6/24/2003

*In the midst of trial and confusion,
I will hold your hand up,
When darkness tries to come,
I will hold your hand up,*

*If my flesh isn't there remember me in spirit,
I will be praying for your strength,
Because our Lord Jesus Christ can fix it,
Our peace cometh from him,*

*So remember when storm clouds rise,
I will be holding your hand,
For every tear you cry,
Remember the footprints in the sand,*

*Whether they are tears of joy,
Or tears of sorrow,
I will hold your hand up,
For joy cometh tomorrow!*

Scripture Reference(s)

Exodus 17:12
(Aaron and Hur held up Moses' hand during a war.)

Poetically Speaking

♦♥♦

About "Holding Up Your Hands"

This was dedicated to my Pastor, because Christ Community vowed to hold her hands up, and I was living on shaky ground. Running in and out of church all the while, keeping Pastor in my prayers. Shoot, there are letters written to God for Pastor, my church, my family and friends even when I felt lost and alone. Being overburdened with doubts and confusion, but never forgetting to talk or write to God when I couldn't fall on my knees and pray. I even joined another church a while ago, but of course Christ Community is my heart so I went back after a couple of months of worshipping with Blessed Hope.

♦♥♦

LaTarsia "Targie" Taylor

A Poem For You – 7/8/2003

When all else seems to fail,
And times get rough,
When your burdens get heavy,
And you've had enough,
Remember God is faithful,
And He watches over you,
Just call out God's name,
He will come to the rescue,
So be encouraged,
With trials at work or home,
For it could be worse,
And you are not alone,
So when the tears are there,
Remember God's will,
Smile, press on,
And say peace be still.

♦♥♦

This poem was dedicated to Mary in her time of bereavement.

Anxious For You – 8/2003

My heart bleeds for you,
Even I don't understand,
I know my feelings are deep,
Just like sinking sand,

From day one my heart cried for you,
Somehow something within me knew,
You were the one God chose for me,
To honor, protect, love, and to marry,
I thank God for bringing us together,
As we grow through stormy weather,

For you my heart leaps filled with joy,
I think about you coming home, oh boy!
I don't know what I would do,
Or how I would react,
I just pray to God,
I don't have a heart attack,
I might leap, jump, kiss and hug you too,
Because I am totally committed to you.

LaTarsia "Targie" Taylor

A Poem For Pastor's Anniversary – 8/3/2003

After 22 years of leading sheep,
Some of us have taken you for granted,
Assuming that leading a flock is easy,
It takes more than faith to stay planted,
From one to numerous sheep through the years,
Some have strayed, but the remnant is still here,
Through our backsliding, and issues too,
You stood your ground and did what God said to do,
We love and appreciate all the things you do,
You are so precious, God's beautiful Angel,
We are so glad that God has chosen you,
To shape & mold us, teaching the truth,
There is no way to make this brief,
Your presence alone is very unique,
Words can't explain a woman so sweet,
So full of God, faith, hope and charity,

May God bless you
Through and through,
We thank you Pastor,
And we love you too.

♦♥♦

Dedicated to Bishop Lillian Robinson-Wiltshire.

Poetically Speaking

<u>*I'll Write It Down - 8/28/2003*</u>

I'll write it down,
Through a letter, poem or song,
I'll write it down,
I'll talk to God if it takes all day long,
I'll write it down,
My heartaches, yes all of the pain,
I'll write it down,
All of my failures even my gains,

I'll write it down,
Yes this filthy mind and body too,
God can cleanse me through and through
Jesus can wash me whiter than snow,
I'll write it down, so the world will know,
That Jesus is my Savior and friend,
If I fall down I can get up again,
God knows I hate the things I do,
I want to live right and to be true.

Scripture Reference(s)

Galatians 6:9 · Ephesians 4:21 - 32

LaTarsia "Targie" Taylor

<u>In The Eyes Of An Usher – 10/17/2003</u>

My heart is for God,
So God I will serve,
With my feet planted,
I will soar like a bird,

My duty is to meet and greet,
I will make sure there is order,
I will escort you to your seat,
In the spirit I'll be caught up,

At times I'll pray you through,
When the spirit allows me to see,
Always know that God loves you,
I am an Usher who has the victory.

Scripture Reference(s)

Psalm 84:10 - 12

"For a day in thy courts is better than a thousand. I had rather be a doorkeeper in the house of my God, than to dwell in the tents of wickedness.

For the Lord God is a sun and shield: the Lord will give grace and glory: no good thing will he withhold from them that walk uprightly.

O Lord of hosts, blessed is the man that trusteth in thee."

Poetically Speaking

The Blood of Jesus - 12/2/2003

How could you try to take over my mind?
When Jesus said I am free,
He died and rose again, remember cavalry?
You can't win this battle,
Not with God on my side,
I trust and love God,
In the name of Jesus Christ,
So leave this home,
Through the blood of Jesus I rebuke you in Jesus' name,
You can't have my body, soul, or mind,
In this house you can't stay,
Father God in the name of your son Jesus,
I pray that we are set free,
Please send your Guardian Angels to watch over me,
Please God let thine will be done,
Please let me write and sing in the name of your son,
I love you God and I mean it too,
Have mercy and forgive me, I want to serve you.

Scripture Reference(s)

Matthew 6 – The Lord's Prayer
Ephesians 6:10 - 20 – The Whole Armor of God

LaTarsia "Targie" Taylor

◆♥◆

About "The Blood of Jesus"

This is one of my, "I need to be free," letters, but I am including it in this book because it seems more like a poem. I was feeling like Paul in Acts. It seemed like the more I tried to do right I would end up doing wrong. This of course is stressful because we are taught not to live in the flesh, but temptation is always there. I guess that's why we are to put on the whole armor of God and do all to stand in the evil day.

◆♥◆

Poetically Speaking

A Spiritual Fall - 2/4/2004

Where do I go? What do I do?
I have strayed away from you,
It's like I don't even care,
But somehow I'm living in fear,
I'm scared of living in sin,
Help me to rise and save me again,
Please forgive my trespasses,
The cursing, smoking, gambling,
Sex and liquor too,
Lord I'm sorry for straying from you,
Father God motivate me again,
God you are my Father and friend,
I need to read the word,
Pray and fast too,
Lord I should be doing
The things you want me to do,
I love you God please guide my way,
Lead me back to you, for too far have I strayed.

Scripture Reference(s)

Proverbs 23 · Proverbs 24

LaTarsia "Targie" Taylor

Restore Me Lord – 3/18/2004

Restore me Lord,
Make me whole again,
You know my circumstance,
Lord you know my sins,
I ask you in Jesus' name,
Please restore my heart again,
This sickness feels like
It's taken a toll on me,
But by your stripes I am healed,
And by faith I am free,
Lord let thine will be done,
Work a miracle on me,
If not let my life be a testimony,
So others will learn and see,
That living in sin will bring you down,
Eating away at you slowly,
Please open a door for me,
Fix my finances set me free,
Please clean out my closet,
Lord a new mind, I stand in need.

Scripture Reference(s)

1 Corinthians 6:19 · James 5:20

Poetically Speaking

Our Road - 3/24/2004

I know these days have been a struggle,
Everywhere we turn, there goes trouble,

But I hope you know that I love you so,
No matter what happens, we can't let go,

Through the fire and through the rain,
Through our issues, heartaches and pain,

We can make it we will survive,
I am your God chosen future wife,

I love you and I miss our laughter,
I pray for peace, from here on after,

I pray for respect, and understanding too,
I hope you can trust me and I can trust you,

May God fill us with unconditional love,
As I send this to you with a kiss and a hug.

LaTarsia "Targie" Taylor

Words of Comfort 3/29/2004

In this life I have learned,
Some blessings are given,
Some are earned,
Some people pass through our lives
For just a season,
Some people suffer more than others,
And we don't know the reason,

Keep your head up,
Rely on God and be strong,
You have a blessed spirit,
You're like a beautiful song,
Remember the good times,
And live for today,
Don't worry about tomorrow,
Or fret over yesterday,

For God has His eyes on the sparrow,
So I know He watches over you,
God will fix all hurt and pain,
Because God's love is true,
Now smile and strut, and don't forget to pray,
Keep on pressing on, and have a blessed day.

♦♥♦

Dedicated to Carmen.

Tax Poem - 3/31/2004

It's tax season again hip, hip, hooray,
I can keep my lights on another day,
My rent will get paid and my gas too,
These are some of the things I want to do,

I will buy myself all new stuff,
Nothing will be the same,
I'll even get my phone turned on,
In my own dag on name,

Isn't this a blimp?
This can't be happening,
The tax preparer told me
That I only get two cents,
All because I don't have kids,
Give me my money,
Man forget dependants,

Well I'm going down to Foster Care,
To get me a child or two,
So next year when I file,
I can get back what's due.

♦♥♦

We had a poetry contest at work and it just happened to be tax season, so I decided to be different and have fun with poetry. Unfortunately, this poem lost the contest. I wonder why!

LaTarsia "Targie" Taylor

I Want to Hold Out – 3/31/2004

Is our love strong?
Can we make it last?
It seems like joy is gone,
And there's no turning back,

I still love you,
But this struggle is stressful,
One day we are cool,
The next day is like screw you,

Can we laugh and joke again?
Can you be my lover and friend?
Will you hold on, as I hold out?
I need to be with God, no doubt!

I want answers
With God as my guide,
I'll have to fast,
And pray putting sin aside.

Poetically Speaking

♦♥♦

About "I Want to Hold Out"

As you already know, in 2002 I made a mistake of allowing a man to live with me. This explains why every other poem was sad or angry. I love God, but I loved this man too and sin was there putting me through a struggle! My mother never lied when she said *"Why buy the cow, when you can get the milk for free?"* I didn't understand it then, but now I'm like, *"Oh yes indeed."* The older folks never lied with that saying, because we lived together for four years before I let it go. Wow, I wish I would've listened. I could have saved myself from a lot of drama. This poem was written because I chose not to have sex anymore and oh my stars did all hell break loose in my home!

♦♥♦

LaTarsia "Targie" Taylor

Pastor's Anniversary - 8/2004

I thank you Lord for Bishop and Elder,
Those two are truly one,
"A family that prays together stays together"
Including their two sons,

A woman standing tall,
Faithful and precious too,
Where she is passive and lenient,
Elder enforces the rules,

A good teacher and preacher,
What more can you ask for?
I thank God, I thank God,
They've shown us the door,

I may not have monetary
Or spiritual gifts to give,
But what I write starts in my heart,
And exits through my lips,

So I thank you God through Jesus,
For showing us the way,
And last but not least,
Pastor, Happy Anniversary!

Poetically Speaking

<u>*A Living Testimony - 2/12/2005*</u>

Jesus I will be a living testimony for thee,
Because you died on cavalry,
And rose again to set me free,
That's why I'll be a mercy vessel for thee,

I will endure the pain,
I will witness to others,
So my trials won't be in vain,
I will always love you,
No I won't be ashamed,
Yes I will praise your Holy name,

I have learned in this life,
That only God can make it right,
So I'll look to Jesus, he is my light,
Holy Spirit please be my guide,
Make me strong so I won't cry,
Lord I am healed by your stripes.

<u>Scripture Reference(s)</u>

Matthew 18:15 - 20

LaTarsia "Targie" Taylor

In Loving Memory of Elder Michael Robinson - 2/24/2005

A man of God, who did not play,
He'd sit and observe, but will have his say,
Yes he listened and would tell you the truth,
He kept eye to eye contact, he wasn't a fool,

He always knew when something was wrong,
He'd tell you to pray, stand up, and be strong,
He gave tough love, with him you had to be straight,
A no nonsense man, no time for the games,

One thing about Elder education was imperative,
If you was in need, yes he would be supportive,
And boy his smile could light up the room,
He loved his family, friends and his food,

I can't speak for everyone,
But I can say as for me, he will be missed greatly,
Because he was a spiritual father to me,
His spirit is with God now, until eternity,
So pick up your head, be strong, and don't weep.

Poetically Speaking

Feeling Trapped 3/2005

There are times I feel trapped,
And times when I feel free,
I know there is someone
Who can and will give me peace,
When I feel like crying
Or I'm angry at someone,
I hear a voice saying,
Call my name and I will come,

When my patience is gone,
And I'm filled with bitterness,
I hear a voice telling me
All about forgiveness,
When I finally stopped
To listen and pray,
God picked me up
And he made my day,

When things go wrong,
And everyone's blaming me,
I will look to my comforter,
The Holy Spirit will protect me.

Scripture Reference(s) – Forgiveness

Mark 11:22 - 26 · Matthew 18:21 - 22
Colossians 3:13

LaTarsia "Targie" Taylor

I Want To Sing – 3/25/2005

I want to sing for Jesus,
Yes bless His holy name,

I want to sing for Jesus,
No I won't be ashamed,

I'm in the process
Of healing my mind,

Body and spirit,
I got the Holy Ghost
On my side,

Yes He will be my guide,
Yes I want to sing for God,
And let the world know,

That if you stay in God,
He will help you grow.

Scripture Reference(s)

Psalm 33 · Psalm 100

Sinking Sand - 7/24/2005

I am writing for joy,
I am writing for peace,
I am writing for victory,
Lord I need to release,
Lord I want to be free,
How do I break the chains?
How can I loose these strongholds?
How can I break free?
Lord help me to tear them down,
Lord free my mind,
Lord give me peace,
Help me Jesus,
To renew my mind,
Give me strength to go on,
Bless me spiritually,
Lord please forgive me,
For all my sins, the ones I know of,
And the ones I don't acknowledge,
Bring me out of the darkness,
Show me the light so I can see,
What you want me to accomplish,
And where you want me to be,
Lord I am slipping, please help to me stand,
I want to be on top, not in sinking sand...

Scripture Reference(s)

Isaiah 43

LaTarsia "Targie" Taylor

The Jesus In Me - 8/6/2005

If I can take one person and make them smile,
Even when they seem to have a big old frown,
That's all right, it's just the Jesus in me,
Letting them know they can still be free,
If I can tell my story and you're going through,
But somehow it touches and enlightens you,
It's all right because that's the Holy Spirit in me,
Letting you know that you too can be free,
If I give you money in your time of need,
Don't feel ashamed, I've been there too,
That's just the Jesus in me shining on you,
If I can comfort you, in the loss of a loved one,
Don't thank me, thank Jesus Christ God's Son,
Because that is the Holy Spirit working in me,
Letting you know that you are free,
If you are able to overcome any type of abuse,
Remember the Holy Spirit is guiding you through,
If for yourself, spouse, or kids
You are able to work, cook and clean,
Remember that's the Holy Trinity,
Moving through you and me.

Scripture Reference(s)

John 14:11 - 19

Poetically Speaking

Jesus Carried The Cross - 8/8/2005

Surely Jesus took up our infirmities,
And carried our sorrows,
We are Holy today,
But backsliders tomorrow,

He was pierced for our transgressions,
And wounded for our iniquities,
But yet and still we are hard headed,
And refuse to get on our knees,

Surely you must feel the pain,
As Jesus was hung on the cross,
It's funny how we are more obedient,
And submissive to our employed boss,

Who by chance has to answer to God too,
So when you are late for church,
But early for work,
Think about who you will have to answer to
When your face kisses the earth.

Scripture Reference(s)

Matthew 19:21 - 26 · Luke 4:4
John 14:1 - 7

LaTarsia "Targie" Taylor

A Young Mother Lost Her Son - 10/2005

In loving memory of you my heart and joy,
I know distance separated us, but you were my baby boy,

I love you regardless of what people say,
We were growing up together and children are hard to raise,

There was no written book, on what I should do,
So I did my best and I have always loved you,

I may not be the easiest to get along with sometimes,
But I want you to know I love you, you were a child of mine,

May God keep you in the hollow of his hands,
You were special and I'm holding on to footprints in the sand,

In the midst of the pain, when sorrow comes,
When all I get is rain and I can't enjoy the sun,

I will call on God, He will fix it, yes, and this is true,
I know He will do it for me, as He watches over you.

♦♥♦

Dedicated to one of my co-workers in the loss of her son.

Oh Lord, Oh Lord - 7/2006

Oh Lord, oh Lord, take away this pain,
I can't see the sun, all I see is rain,
Oh Lord, Oh Lord, lift my burden now,
This load is wearing me down,

Oh Lord, Oh Lord, the man done broke my heart
Lord I should've loved you from the start,
Oh Lord, Oh Lord, I can't take this pain,
Lord this sickness is driving me insane,

Oh Lord, Oh Lord, where is my faith?
Lord I'm sorry let me not complain,
You brought me through worse times than this,
So if anyone can, I know you can fix it,

I'll hold on, and stay in your way,
Yes I will serve you Lord forever and a day.

My day of freedom came on 7/8/06 at night when the straw broke the camel's back in my relationship. It was over after dating on and off for years, then living together for four years. Believe it or not, I did not shed a tear. Don't get me wrong I was hurt, but I think I was overcome with so much anger that I didn't give myself room to vent. God hardened my heart so that I would have strength to go on.

LaTarsia "Targie" Taylor

Missing Canarsie Blues - 6/8/2007

I complained about the girls and boys,
Shoot, some of them needed a smack,
I complained of the noise,
But now I want it back,

I complained about staff too,
I complained of the commute,
But what I wouldn't give to ride,
On transit to Canarsie's side,

Yes, I have the missing Canarsie's blues,
Maybe someday we will meet again soon,
Yes, Cluster 3, I love you too,
No other cluster,
Can rock like we rule.

♦♥♦

The Canarsie Library closed for renovations and I became a floating Technical Resource Specialist. With the exception of one or two, I really missed my work buddies.

Poetically Speaking

<u>Get Right - 7/2007</u>

At a loss for words,
What can I say?
You can't change tomorrow,
What you did today,

Live right be fair,
That's all you can do,
You made your bed,
Now it's up to you,

How are you living?
Is your mind right?
Are you true to yourself?
Are you walking in the light?

<u>Scripture Reference(s)</u>

Matthew 11:28 - 30

LaTarsia "Targie" Taylor

Chavone's Beloved Grandma – 7/2007

As I sleep in peace,
Try to hold on for me,
Our Father has called me home,
So I am far from being alone,
After years of trials and pain,
I feel the sun after the rain,
Oh yeah, I've had joy and laughter too,
Now you must live and make it through,
Yes most family rivals were settled by me,
But just love each other, and live in peace,
Pray, get along and stay together,
Love conquers all kinds of weather,
Peace opens the door for love,
I will be watching from Heaven above,
I know that times are changing,
And yours and mine are not the same,
But remember my wisdom,
And always call on Jesus' name,
Last but not least don't weep for me,
Shout hallelujah, because I am free,
I can talk, walk, and think,
For I have my victory!

Poetically Speaking

<u>Oh Lord, Slipping Again!</u>

Oh Lord,
Did I do it again?
Succumb to temptation,
Satan is here
To kill and destroy,
What was I thinking?
Boy, oh boy,
The enemy will use
Your work and your home,
Using your family and friends,
So you will feel alone,
Boy oh boy,
Lord help me now,
I have learned my lesson,
I am your child,
Oh Lord I love you,
I don't want to serve idols,
I just want to serve you,
because your agape love is true.

Scripture Reference(s)

Galatians 3:10 · Psalm 51 · Matthew 9

LaTarsia "Targie" Taylor

My Beloved Aunt Betty - 7/17/2007

A loving lady who welcomed all in,
Whether you were family or a friend,
Love is what she gave,
Not standing for any jive,
Oh no, she couldn't stand a lie,
She would tell you like it is,
Yes she would flip her wig,
Love is what she gave,
Sometimes we felt betrayed,
During our ups and downs,
When all in all we needed to turn around,
Tough love is hard to understand,
Our actions deal us some very rough hands,
This woman held her head up high
Even though her heart was torn up inside,
She has overcome many storms,
Trials and tribulations,
She has raised and mentored so many
She might have created a nation,
Yes she will be missed,
Yes she is well loved,
Yes she is free now,
In her home above.

Poetically Speaking

<u>A Storm In The Hallway - 11/08/2007</u>

Whenever God closes a door,
He will and can open many more,

Even though hell is going on,
God will see you through your storm,

So if you are going to worry, don't pray,
Because the storm is in the hallway,

God said walk by faith and not by sight,
So hold on everything is going to be all right,

There's a storm in the hallway,
But don't worry, just pray,

God will guide you always,
So be strong and hold on to faith.

<u>Scripture Reference(s)</u>

Act 27:14 - 26 · Matthew 7:7 · Matthew 8:23 - 27
Revelation 3:20

LaTarsia "Targie" Taylor

<u>Stop Judging – 11/2007</u>

Don't destroy a dove on distant oaks,
Don't pull the trigger killing someone's hope,

For their Judge is the Lily of the Valley,
But your judgments pushed them in an alley,

God is our judge so whom shall we fear?
Ask God for peace and ears to hear,

So you'll be slow to talk and quick to listen,
Maybe it's not the accused,
But it's you who needs to be disciplined.

<u>Scripture Reference(s) - Judgmental People</u>

Matthew 7:1 – 5 · John 8:3 - 11

Poetically Speaking

<u>50 + 50 = 100% of *Love* - 11/28/2007</u>

My love for you
Will never die
I feel it within
Yes deep down inside
Smile for me
It fills my soul
Only you Baby
Can make me whole
50 of you
50 of me
Gives me a reason
To want to breathe
100% of a love
So true
Half of me
Half of you
So smile for me
Even though we're apart
I love you, Baby
So catch my heart
And don't ever let go
Because you're the man
That makes me whole.
Love your Baby Girl, 50 + 50 = 100%, soul mates forever,
don't you ever forget.

LaTarsia "Targie" Taylor

Right Back at You – 12/10/2007

To truly speak is to express
What words cannot do,
But if you ask me
I truly love you,

Time has told our story
And only you stop my worry,
I gave my heart,
Mind, body, and soul,
For you to cherish
And always hold,

Words cannot speak
But through expression you will see,
Just how much you mean
And have meant to me!!!

Poetically Speaking

◆♥◆

About *"Right Back at You"*

This was dedicated to me in response to the "50 + 50 = 100% of Love" poem that I wrote to my first carnal love. I don't know, but we always end up closer to each other when we are going through storms in life. I will set the record straight. I never cheated on my live-in love for all of those years. I have always been in contact with my first, but it was really friendship. After 2007 I fell hard for him, but a wall is there physically and emotionally. I don't know where we are supposed to go from here. Besides, jail talk will make you believe the sky isn't blue. Loneliness can make you open up like a receptacle. So every other letter is a love and war thing. I don't want to mess up my relationship with God anymore so I ask that his will be done in our lives. I want God to choose my mate, not my flesh. I have been on too many familiar roads like this before. I am very skeptical.

◆♥◆

LaTarsia "Targie" Taylor

When Life Seems Unbearable - 1/8/2008

When care is pressing you down a bit,

and life seems so full of discouragement,

When the days are just passing by,

and every moment you have to sigh,

When it seems like life is unbearable,

That's when God will send an angel,

To lead, guide and comfort you,

For God's love is ever so true,

Just call on his name,

Don't give up,

Or feel ashamed,

for God will wash every tear away,

Because God is love forever and a day.

Scripture Reference(s)

Psalm 91

Poetically Speaking

In The Loss Of Genelle's Father - 1/10/2008

No one can understand the loss you've encountered,

No one can replace the comfort of your father,

No one can tell you how you feel,

Only you know what is really real,

No one can bring back a soul resting in peace,

No one can erase any of your memories,

Through your ups and downs,

Through your smiles and frowns,

Somehow you made it, still standing tall,

So that means you are virtuous after all,

May God be with you all day long,

For when you are weak, God is strong.

LaTarsia "Targie" Taylor

In The Loss Of Sheneqia's Cousin - 1/10/2008

In your time of mourning,

I will hold your hand,

I will try to listen,

And I will try to understand,

In your time of mourning,

I will be there for you,

I'll cook you food and pray

For God to bring you through,

In your time of mourning,

I will try to make you laugh,

Because God is love,

And I'm the weirdest friend you have.

Poetically Speaking

Forgive Me God – 2008

I apologize for disappointing you,

And not standing up for what I believe,

I love you Lord you are all I need,

I know you love me God,

And when the pressure is on,

I must not give in,

I want to be strong,

I want to hold on,

Jesus died and rose again,

So that we will be free from sin,

So please help me stand in the evil day,

Please cleanse & help wash my sins away.

Scripture Reference(s)

Proverbs 24:16 · 2 Corinthians 12:9

♦♥♦

Since Jesus was tempted, why would we be exempt? (Luke 4)

LaTarsia "Targie" Taylor

I Want To Make Changes - 4/2008

I want to make changes,
In my life for you,
I want to make changes,
For you'll see me through,
Lord I'm tired of sin alone,
I want to be perfect,
Or at least a little close,
With you all things are possible,
I am claiming my change,
Through the Holy Ghost,
These days are going by fast,
Lord I know in sin I won't last,
So I'm changing my life around,
I want to walk with you on holy ground,
Yes you've seen my tears and heard my cries,
Yes you've seen me fall and get up by and by.

Scripture Reference(s)

Isaiah 64:6 · Proverbs 24:16 - 20

Poetically Speaking

Turned Inside Out – 11/20/2009

The devil came to steal, kill, and destroy,
So why did I allow him to steal my joy?
Greater is He that is in me,
Than he that is in the world,
I would rather be free,
Than to be spun in a swirl,
Torn and beaten, feeling abused,
I fell in a trap, now I feel used,
My family and friends or are they my foes?
I am sitting in sorrow dwelling on my woes,
Where is my faith? Is God still there?
My heart feels numb, is love still here?
I allowed the devil to turn me inside out,
Do I give up, pray, run, scream, or shout?
I have fallen mentally, which is killing me physically,
But if I turn around I will see,
That God is and has never left me,
Yes God loves me and He cares,
So help me Lord, I know you are there,
Take away my pain, misery, and fears,
Yes I am turned inside out,
But God can save me without a doubt,
I must find my way back right now,
I must love again, someway, somehow.

LaTarsia "Targie" Taylor

The Oak Tree - 12/08/2009

A mighty wind
blew night and day,
It stole the oak tree's leaves away,
then snapped its boughs, And pulled its bark,
until the oak was tired and stark, But still the oak
tree held its ground, while other trees fell all around,
The weary wind gave up and spoke, "how can you still be
standing oak?" The oak tree said "I know that you, can
break each branch of mine in two, carry every leaf
away, shake my limbs, and make me sway, but I have
roots
Stretched in the earth,
Growing stronger
Since my birth,
You'll never touch them
For you see they are the deepest part of me...

♦♥♦

This was dedicated to me by my first carnal love. I was going through some storms and told him *"I am weak and I can't go on."* In response he sent me an inspirational letter along with this poem. Thanks a million. Love you always.

To All My Aunts - 1/6/2010

May God guide your ways,

And fill you with more love today,

I pray you enough joy to last a lifetime,

I pray you enough peace in the light,

Thank you for caring and loving me too,

Thank you for an open heart that's true,

I love you just because,

You are like God's precious doves,

May God bless you,

Yes this simple prayer will do.

LaTarsia "Targie" Taylor

<u>My Sistah Girls - 1/6/2010</u>

Hey ladies you know who you are,
Whether you are near or far,
Thanks for being there to listen to me,
When I was complaining or just happy,
Every tear I've shed and you shed them with me,
Every argument, our pains and miseries,
The spades games, drinking and partying too,
Wow, I won't tell all the things we used to do,
Through prayer and supplication,
We have created a nation,
Of strong Black Queen's,
With God first overcoming everything,
My friends, my sistahs, yes I love you,
May God keep us bonded and true,
Yes my sistahs pray for me as I pray for you.

Poetically Speaking

<u>My Cousins - 1/6/2010</u>

Truly I am thankful for the laughs we share,
Yes I am thankful that you love me and care,

I want to say thank you for just being there,
Whether it was physical or you lending an ear,

I ask that God increases your strength & wealth,
May you be the best and always be there to help,

A family that prays together stays together,
Remember after the storm it will get better,

Yes my cousins, my cousins I love you,
Don't ever change and to God be true.

LaTarsia "Targie" Taylor

Abusive Breakdown - 1/7/2010

Mentally you are tearing me down,
I want your loving, but you aren't around,
Your words are cruel, and I sense deception,
I am caught up on a wheel of deadly rejection,

Physically your hands are all over me,
Choking, poking, slapping, pushing me fiercely,
Why? Why? Why me? The aches & pains,
If I stay I'll surely die, no I'm not insane,

Sexually you force yourself on me,
I don't want to be here in misery,
Is this what this has come down to,
You using me and me hating you?

I know there's a way, yes I can escape,
Right now I will fall down on my knees to pray,
It's over now, I vow to stand,
It is over, I have God's hand,
It is over, I love myself more,
I am worthy of love, God has opened the door.

ABUSE - 1/7/2010

Abuse in any shape, form, or fashion,
Is wrong and unhealthy, so take action,
Don't live in denial, making excuses,
Stop saying it's you, or how it was due,

Take a stand dear woman or man,
Where is your self-esteem?
Love yourself again, be free,
Build up your faith,
Pray each and every day,
For God will make a way,
Yes you can escape,

Trust & submit unto God,
For His way is not hard,
Wipe your tears, smile again,
Jesus loves you, you can win,
Pray for protection & strength,
You are strong like a lion,
So be brave and be proud,
Yes peace will be still after awhile.

LaTarsia "Targie" Taylor

Cry Me A River - 1/17/2010

Cry me a river, for my heart bleeds
My uncle has gone to Heaven and now he is free

Cry me a river, because his smile was bright
He was outgoing and loving, a tropical sunlight

Cry me a river, for words cannot explain,
The rhythm of music, oh boy could he sing,
A voice so powerful, yet tender and smooth,
His songs filled your ears with rhythm & blues
Telling a story as life unfolds,
A voice now heard on Heaven's road,

Weeping may endureth for a night,
But joy cometh in the morning light,
As we look towards the hills from where our help comes from,
We will see the river of tears filled by love, so peace shall come.

♦♥♦

In loving memory of my Uncle Derek (KERED)

Poetically Speaking

<u>Hold On My Sister - 2/24/2010</u>

Yes life seems to deal us unfair hands,
Yes it feels like we are sinking in sand,
Yes sometimes you cry and scream,
But with God we can do all things,

My strong sister yes you are a queen,
Change will come, because you are free,
Your struggles aren't for naught or in vain,
Remember the blessings come after the rain,

So press on and smile,
This is just a trial,
You can make it,
My sister you can take it,
Only the strong survive,
You can still fight,
So smile and stay true,
Hey Big Sis I love you.

Dedicated to Kim.

LaTarsia "Targie" Taylor

Letting Go, And Letting God - 2/24/2010

Don't let trials and tribulations wear you down,

There are times of celebration and calamity all around,

Yes sometimes we laugh and sometimes we cry,

Sometimes we take it sometimes we complain and ask why,

We ask for things and wait on answers time after time,

Throwing temper tantrums & rebelling losing our minds,

We have to shed slowly, decreasing as God increases in us,

Renewing our minds, being slow to talk learning not to fuss,

Experience will give you patience, strength, and faith too,

For you will grow stronger as you get over every obstacle,

Believe it and receive it, your road doesn't have to be hard,

So press & hold on my people, by letting go and letting God.

I guess it wasn't that bad if you have made it to the end. Thank you for going on a *Poetic Journey* of my life with me. I pray that God blesses you abundantly. I pray that God gives you a refreshed heart, mind, and spirit in the name of Jesus, by the power of the Holy Ghost. I pray that you have gained more spiritual knowledge through some of the scriptures. Sometimes when we think we are going through hell in hot water and we just want to give up, someone will come with a story to tell and make your woes look like you have good luck. Keep your eyes on God because He will never leave nor forsake you. Sometimes the road we choose can set off a destiny for us that we think we can't handle, but just hold on there is always a blessing after the storm. You can do all things through Christ who strengthens you. Let go and let God. He will make a way out of no way just for you.

Father God in the name of Jesus by the power of the Holy Spirit please touch and agree with us right now as we pray for peace in our homes, jobs, and everywhere we travel. God give us wisdom and knowledge so we can grow in truth. God, please deliver us from evil and forgive our sins. God you know we are striving to make it in. Only you can bring us through it. God we know that you hold all power in your hand, so we will hold on and for you we will stand. Thank you God for a closer walk with you! Thank you for everything you have done and for all that will come to pass. Thank you God Almighty we are free at last.

Special Thanks

My Spiritual "Aunt-Moms" Mama Cyrus and Minister Renee Wells. You are a combination of a Mom mixed with an Aunt spiritually to me so I just made up a title for you. Love you much.

For some blessed, custom-designed, made from scratch desserts, check out Cheenky's Cakes! A doll, a butterfly...you name it..she'll make it. Go Chema! Facebook her @ Chema Cheenky Taylor.

To my spiritual brother James Robinson/Yung Chef. I hope you find the perfect place to utilize your culinary skills. Pray and I believe God will place you in the restaurant that is in His will. Love you brother and may peace be still.

A genuine shout out to the Liverpools in Maryland. Thanks for loving me and taking me in as a blood relative when I was living out there.

Special acknowledgement for my sister girl Author Rebecca Greene. I really loved all of your books please continue writing because you are truly blessed. Please visit: www.rebeccasbooks.com.

A special shout out to my spiritual Brother Shaun Gabriel @ http://berettamusicworld.com/shaun/beretta.html. Good luck on your music CD that just dropped. You know I already have mine. May you continue to let God lead you and be encouraged no matter what comes your way.

Official Burn's CD: *Destroy By Fire* available on iTunes. Keep up the good work.

Much love to my brothers Jimmie, Obed, and Rodney.

Special love for Aunt Holly & Honey. Thanks for your daily inspirational words of encouragement.

Sending my love to the Brooklyn Public Library staff and patrons!

To My Other Mothers: "My Godmother Donna Williams, Jana Cooke, Janet Hoyte, Otelia Liverpool, Vera Alston, Gail & June Duncan, Bishop Lillian Robinson-Wiltshire my spiritual Mom, and Delores Moore."

Paulette (Lou) Williams, I know you are Chema's godmother and like an aunt to us, but I will never forget that you were there in my mother's place for my high school graduation.

Hi Leon! Even though you are my cousin, you felt more like a dad to me while I was living in Maryland. LOL! Love you much.

To My Grandmothers: Odessa Taylor, Susie Workman, Vivian Moore and Susanna Baptiste.

Grandpa: Donnell Workman & R.I.P. Granddaddy Jesse Taylor

To My Little Sistah: "Kash," many blessings on your album, "Kalling All Soldiers Home." I wish you much success.

My Baby Sisters: ShaVantae & ShaDante Bonner love you much!

To My Sistah Girls: Tawanna, Monique, ShaKeeba, Sheneqia, Satydra, Tara, Genelle, Krista, Tiffany, Camille, Chavone, NaKeema, LeCarsha, Taisha, Team Evil, my HSTAT & BPL sistahs.

Dedicated to all my blood, and spiritual cousins who are really there for me constantly right now in my life, whether to hear me vent (rarely I know I have to stop holding everything in), giving me rides, praying for me, or laughing at my silly jokes: ShaKema, Shauntia, Tyree, Tamika, Armani, SheKieta, Dominique, Wednesday, Chris, Des, Shanecka, Tobi, Teri, Muff, Vicki, Tasha, Shaun, Kettie, Shanita, Twana, and many more to name, but you know who you are, some of you are a pain in the neck, but I love you anyway. I really believe all my cousins love me and will support me always.

By blood, marriage, and in spirit: The Taylors, Kings, Millers, Kingsberrys, Lockes, Fortes, Robinsons, Murdocks, Thomases, Draytons, Workmans, Moores, Hoytes, Keiths and everybody else that loves me as their own blood.

If your name is not mentioned, please know that I have not forgotten you. Smooches, and love on earth and above.

Author Biography

LaTarsia "Targie" Taylor was born and raised on the tough streets of Brooklyn, New York. Her mother held down the fort by raising three young baby girls alone. When Targie was 16 years old her mother passed away, leaving them to face the world without her protection, words of comfort or reassuring smile. Her relief from pain & trials is the love of God, writing songs, poems, and short stories hoping that someone will be set free, especially herself.

Coming Soon!

Targie's Way of...Daily Meditations
My way of coping with life on a daily basis.

Contact Information:
LaTarsia "Targie" Taylor
E-mail: Targie2010@gmail.com
Website: www.targietaylor.com